ACT WORD GAMES

Michele R. Wells

LEARNINGEXPRESS ®

NEW YORK

Library of Congress Cataloging-in-Publication Data

Wells, Michele R.
  ACT word games / Michele R. Wells — 1st ed.
     p. cm.
  ISBN-13: 978-1-57685-797-7
  ISBN-10: 1-57685-797-2
  1. Word games. 2. ACT Accessment. I. Title.
  GV1507.W8W355 2011
  793.734—dc22

                  2011012656

Printed in the United States of America

9 8 7 6 5 4 3 2 1

First Edition

ISBN 978-1-57685-797-7

For more information or to place an order, contact LearningExpress at:
  2 Rector Street
  26th Floor
  New York, NY 10006

Or visit us at:
  www.learnatest.com

About the Author

Michele R. Wells has been a writer and editor of test prep materials for companies such as The Princeton Review and LearningExpress, LLC, since 2001, and volunteers regularly with the Everybody WINS Power Lunch program, a NYC-based literacy program for kids. A senior editor at one of the world's largest publishing companies, she has more than a decade of experience in nonfiction book and multimedia publishing. Michele holds a bachelor's degree in dramatic writing and art history, and is pursuing a master's in film, both from New York University.

Acknowledgments ▶

Jennifer Pollock, editor extraordinaire, conceptualized the idea for this book and deserves a big thank you. Thanks also to Sheryl Posnick, who not only edited but dealt with various obstacles to make sure that this book came together as it should. Additional thanks to Eric Titner, production editor at LearningExpress, who worked to make this book the best it could be.

Andrea Laurencell is in the trenches, teaching vocabulary and test preparation to students every day. *Merci* to you for reviewing the manuscript, and for your feedback and advice.

And finally, writing two books in six months is difficult. Thanks to my family (Rita Sr., Rita Jr., Cheryl, John, Nathan, Colby, and Blake) for understanding where my priorities had to be this year.

Table of Contents

Introduction ▶

If you've picked up this book, you're interested in increasing your ACT score. That means you're already aware of the effect this exam can have on your future, and that's great. But you've also got homework to do, football games to attend, musical instruments and Spanish verbs to practice, chores to do, maybe an after-school job and other responsibilities, and—oh yeah—a social life to maintain. You don't have time to spend on more stuff related to school, much less exams that are probably months away at this point, right?

But think about it like this: You probably play games of some kind or another, either on your mobile phone, computer, or a game console, several times a week—maybe even every day. Playing those games can increase your online ranking, and maybe even make your friends jealous when you beat their high scores, but playing the games in this book can have a positive effect on your future. They can help you build a killer vocabulary and put yourself on stronger ground for gaining admission to the college of your choice.

Before we get to just how these games can help increase your ACT scores, let's run through a bit about the test itself, so you'll know exactly what to expect on test day.

What Is the ACT Exam?

The American College Testing (ACT) assessment is one of two main standardized tests used by admissions teams to evaluate your potential fit as a student at their college or university. The ACT measures what you've learned in various academic subjects—see "What Skills Are Tested on the ACT?" for more information. (The other main standardized test is the SAT, which is an aptitude exam designed to measure the verbal and mathematical skills you will need as you progress through your academic career.)

What Is the ACT Used For?

Your high school may use your ACT score to evaluate the way your teachers are performing. They use these scores to decide which areas need improvement within the school as a whole, and which students need additional assistance in specific subject areas.

College admissions teams use your ACT score as part of their evaluation process, to decide if you will be a good addition to the diverse group of students at that school. But that's not the only thing they look at.

Admissions teams look at individuals, not just at scores and grades. They want well-rounded students, not just those who can churn out perfect tests or straight As. Are you an athlete? Maybe you're an actor or dancer? How about an artist? Do you do volunteer work, speak another language, or organize events for your school? Make sure you mention all these things on your application, because admissions teams are looking for students who can contribute to the diversity of campus life.

Don't worry if your GPA isn't perfect—just be sure to highlight the great work you do in other areas of your life. And with the help of this book, your English, reading, and writing ACT scores are sure to be included in the "things you do well" section!

What Skills Are Tested on the ACT?

The ACT is a national achievement and placement exam that tests your knowledge of key subject areas: English, mathematics, reading, and science. The optional ACT Plus Writing assessment also includes a 30-minute essay test that evaluates your writing skills.

The English section is made up of 75 multiple-choice questions. The mathematics section comprises 60 questions. The reading and science sections are made up of 40 questions each. The optional writing section consists of a short essay on a particular theme. Overall, the exam takes a little over four hours to complete (with an additional half-hour if you choose to take the ACT Plus Writing assessment).

Who Takes the ACT?

According to the American College Testing Program, Inc., the organization that administers the ACT, approximately 1.6 million students take the ACT every year. But here's a little secret—not all of them prepare for the exam in advance. By using this book, you're giving yourself an edge over the competition!

Where Do I Sign Up for the ACT?

Registration forms and information for the ACT exam can be found online at www.actstudent.org. You can sign up for the ACT online with a credit card or request a paper application, which you can complete and mail in with a check or money order.

When Do I Take the ACT?

The ACT exam is administered six times a year, on Saturday mornings. You can find a current schedule online at www.actstudent.org/regist/dates.html. You may take the ACT up to twelve times—but only once per national test date. Most students take the test twice: once as a high school junior, and once as a senior. According to the American College Testing Program, Inc., among the students who took the ACT more than once, 55 percent increased their composite score on the retest.

Where Do I Take the ACT?

You can take the ACT in one of many national and international testing centers. When you register by mail or at www.actstudent.org, you'll be given a list of testing locations in the area of your choosing; just pick the one that is most comfortable and convenient for you. It's also a good idea to do a dry run before the actual test date—figure out how you'll get to the test site around the same time of day as your test so you aren't surprised by road closures, construction, train or bus delays, bad on-line directions, or other things that can make you late (and stress you out) the day of the test.

If there is no ACT exam center within 50 miles of your home, if your religious beliefs prohibit you from taking tests on a Saturday, or if you are homebound or confined, you may request arranged testing. Information on these arrangements can be found at www.actstudent .org/regist under "Request arranged testing."

How Is the ACT Scored?

The first thing that happens after you take the ACT is that your multiple-choice answers are calculated into a score by computer. Points are awarded as follows: For the English, mathematics, reading, and science reasoning sections, one point is added for each correct answer (nothing is subtracted for incorrect answers), for a score between 1 and 36. The English, mathematics, and reading tests will also include subscores ranging from 1 to 18. These scores are averaged for a composite score.

If you choose to take the optional writing test, that section will be scored manually by two trained readers. You'll receive a writing score that falls between 2 and 12 (or 0 if your essay is blank, illegible, off-topic, not written with a No. 2 pencil, or written in a language other than English), for a combined English and writing score of between 1 and 36, and comments from the essay scorers. Your writing score will have no effect on your composite score.

How Is My Score Reported?

You can view your scores online at www.actstudentorg if you have a student account and tested through National or International Testing (see the ACT website for more information). Scores are available online approximately two and a half weeks after you complete the test. If you chose to take the ACT Plus Writing assessment, your writing scores will be posted online approximately two weeks after your multiple-choice scores appear. Score reports are also mailed to your home address three to eight weeks after you complete the test (or after your writing scores have been calculated if you took the ACT Plus Writing assessment).

Your ACT scores will be sent to the colleges or universities you authorize for score reports. You can also opt to have your scores sent to your high school by checking "yes" in the registration section.

How Does My Score Rate?

In 2010, the national average ACT composite score was 21. This average score is acceptable for many colleges and universities. Some schools, such as Ivy League universities, typically require a score of at least 29.

The highest possible score on the ACT is 36. Typically, less than one-tenth of one percent of all students who take the ACT receive a score of 36. Keep in mind that your score is just one of the tools used by admissions officers to rate your potential fit for that school.

What Are the Subscores?

Subscores on the ACT are broken down into the following categories: usage/mechanics and rhetorical skills for English; pre-algebra/elementary algebra, algebra/geometry, and plane geometry/trigonometry for mathematics; and social studies/sciences and arts/literature for reading. These subscores provide you with greater detail on your performance, to show you the areas in which you need to improve; however, they are not used for college admissions purposes.

What's the Deal with National Rankings?

Your score report will also include national rankings. These show the percentage of recent high school graduates who took the ACT and scored at or below each of your scores. These rankings are included to give you a sense of your strengths and weaknesses in each of the four general subject areas tested on the ACT, and in each of the seven sub-score sections.

What If I Didn't Get the Score I Wanted?

You can always retest if you don't do as well as you'd have liked on the ACT—in fact, you can take the exam up to twelve times. But unlike the SAT, which allows you to hide your lowest scores, all your official ACT test scores will appear on the score reports that are sent out to approved colleges and universities.

Now that you know what the exam is, how it is used, and what to expect on test day, let's get down to what you really want to know—how to use this book to get great results on the ACT.

I

UNDERSTAND BASIC VOCABULARY SECRETS

1 ▶ Know Your Common Prefixes and Suffixes

Knowing the meaning of common prefixes and suffixes will help you figure out the definition of many familiar and unfamiliar words on the ACT exam.

What Exactly Are Prefixes and Suffixes?

Prefixes and suffixes are attached to base words to add information and meaning. A **prefix** is an attachment that comes *before* a base word or stem. A **suffix** is an attachment that comes *after* the existing base word or stem. A **stem** is the main part of a word—the part that prefixes or suffixes are attached to—but might not actually be a full word by itself.

The word *repayment*, for example, is made up of the prefix *re-* (which means *again*), the stem *pay*, and the suffix *-ment* (which means *action* or *process*). So with an understanding of suffix, prefix, and stems, you could figure out that the meaning of *repayment* is *the process of paying money back.*

Common Prefixes

The following are some examples of prefixes you might encounter when studying ACT vocabulary words, along with their meanings.

a-, *ab-*, *an-* (apart or without)

ad- (toward or near)

ante- (before)

anti- (against)

auto- (self)

bi- (two)

bio- (life)

circum- (around)

co-, *com-*, *con-* (with or together)

de- (away or off)

di-, *dis-* (not or apart)

dys- (bad or problematic)

em-, *en-* (restrict or cause)

equi- (equal)

ex- (former)

extra-, *exo-* (outside of)

fore- (in front of or before)

hyper- (over)

hypo- (under)

geo- (earth)

im-, *in-* (not)

inter- (between)

micro- (tiny)

mis- (wrong)

mono- (one)

multi- (many)

neo- (new)

non- (not)

ob-, *oc-*, *of-*, *op-* (against, on, over, or toward)

omni- (all)

pan- (all)

para- (beyond)

peri- (around or about)

poly- (many)

post- (after)

pre- (before)

pro- (favoring or for)

re- (again)

retro- (backward)

semi- (half)

sub- (under or below)

super- (exceeding or above)

therm-, *thermo-* (heat)

trans- (across)

tri- (three)

un- (not)

Common Suffixes

-able, *-ible* (capable or worthy of)

-acy (state or quality)

-age (condition)

-al (act or process of, or pertaining to)

-ance, *-ence* (state or quality)

-ary (related to)

-ate (become)

-dom (place or state of being)

-en (make or become)

-er, *-or* (one who)

-esque (like or reminiscent of)

-gram, *-graph* (written or drawn)

-hood (class)

-ic, -ical (pertaining to)

-iou, -ous (characterized by)

-ish (having the quality of)

-ive (having the nature of)

-less (without)

-log, -logue (speech)

-logy (the study of)

-oid (resembles)

-ory, -tory (relating to)

-ous (possessing)

-phile (strong love for)

-phobe, -phobia (fear of)

-ship (position held)

-y (characterized by)

WORD DETECTIVE

Knowing these prefixes and suffixes can help you deduce the meaning of many vocabulary words instantly, so familiarize yourself with the ones you don't already know for an instant vocab power-up!

Derivational Suffixes

There are suffixes that change the meaning of the base word or stem. These are called **derivational suffixes** (don't worry, you don't need to remember that), and some common examples are:

-able, -ible (capable of being)

-ation, -sion, -tion (state of being)

-ful (notable for)

-fy (make or become)

-ify (make or become)

-ily

-ise, -ize (become)

-ism (belief or doctrine)

-ist (one who)

-ity, -ty (having the quality of)

-ment (condition or result of)

-ness (state of being)

Derivational suffixes can combine with each other, too, but the spelling may change (as in *predictability*, which is *predict* combined with *-able* and *-ity*).

Okay, now that you've reviewed some prefixes and suffixes and how they work, let's put that knowledge into action!

Exercise 1

Each word below contains a prefix. Using what you learned, choose the best available definition.

1. microcosm
   a. to make something larger
   b. a sign of fear
   c. a smaller system which is representative of a larger one
   d. a vast expanse of land

2. foreshadow
   a. to darken
   b. to suggest something in advance
   c. to follow
   d. to retaliate

3. engender
   a. to bring into existence; to cause
   b. knowledge
   c. to promise to marry
   d. to grow

4. commingle
   a. to bring forward
   b. to mix or blend
   c. a quick movement
   d. to soften

5. extraordinary
   a. from the past
   b. exceptional or unusual
   c. from above
   d. large

Exercise 2

Each word below contains a suffix. Using what you learned, choose the best available definition.

1. historical
   a. dry
   b. extremely funny
   c. something that belongs to a man
   d. relating to what happened in the past

2. provenance
   a. place or source of origin
   b. a gift
   c. the act of being proper or correct
   d. happiness

3. fiefdom
   a. a type of instrument
   b. unhappiness
   c. a domain controlled by a dominant person or lord
   d. a small area

4. travelogue
   a. a vacation
   b. a language
   c. confrontation
   d. the journal or documentation of a trip

5. humanoid
   a. resembling or having the characteristics of a human
   b. false or fake
   c. a very young person
   d. an alien

Exercise 3

Each word below contains a prefix and a suffix or derivational suffix. Using what you learned, choose the best available definition.

1. decentralize
    a. to cause to be more populated
    b. in the very middle of an area
    c. to move downward
    d. to move away from an established main point

2. monograph
    a. a work of writing on a single subject
    b. a diverse group
    c. a drawing made with many colors
    d. a signature

3. apprehension
    a. to climb
    b. fearful expectation
    c. a course that comes before a meal
    d. the state of being angry

4. nullify
    a. to take apart
    b. to make invalid
    c. to bring together
    d. to make liquid

5. approbation
    a. a decision
    b. restriction
    c. concern
    d. official approval

Answers

Exercise 1

1. **c**. a smaller system which is representative of a larger one
2. **b**. to suggest something in advance
3. **a**. to bring into existence; to cause
4. **b**. to mix or blend
5. **b**. exceptional or unusual

Exercise 2

1. **d**. relating to what happened in the past
2. **a**. place or source of origin
3. **c**. domain controlled by a dominant person or lord
4. **d**. the journal or documentation of a trip
5. **a**. resembling or having the characteristics of a human

Exercise 3

1. **d**. move away from an established main point
2. **a**. work of writing on a single subject
3. **b**. fearful expectation
4. **b**. make invalid
5. **d**. official approval

2 ▶ Learn Root Words

Now that you know the meanings that prefixes and suffixes bring to vocabulary words, you're ready to review the most common **roots**—the base of the words to which prefixes and suffixes are attached. Once you know these, you can guess the meaning of almost any unfamiliar word on the ACT exam.

Root Words

English is made up of words derived from Latin and Greek roots, as well as words from German, French, and other languages. Any familiarity you have with other languages can be an advantage when trying to guess the meaning of a word, because if you can recognize even a small part of it, you've improved your chances of figuring out the definition.

List of Common Root Words

acro (top, height, tip)

aer, aero (air)

aesth, esth (beauty)

agr, agri, agro (farm)

alg, algo (pain)

ambi, amphi (both)

ambul (move)

ami, amo (love)

andr, andro (male)

anim (spirit, life)

ann, enn (year)

anth, antho (flower)

anthrop, anthropo (human)

  apo, apho (away, separate)

aqu, aqua (water)

arbor (tree)

arch (most important)

archa, archae, archi (ancient)

art (skill)

arthr, arthro (joint)

aster, astr (star)

act (to do)

audi (to hear)

avi (bird)

bar, baro (pressure)

bell, belli (war)

bene (good)

bibli (book)

bio (life)

blast (cell)

capt, cept (capture, hold)

cardi, cardio (heart)

carn, carni (flesh)

caust, caut (burn)

cede, ceed (yield)

ceive, cept (take)

celer (fast)

cent, centi (hundred)

centr, centro (center)

cephal, cephalo (head)

chrom, chromo, chromat,

  chromato (color)

cide, cise (cut)

circle, circum (around)

claim, clam (speak)

cline (lean)

cogn, cogni (learn)

cred (believe)

crypto (hidden)

cycl (circle)

dem, demo (people)

dendr, dendri, dendro (tree)

dent, dont (tooth)

derm, derma (skin)

dic, dict (speak)

domin (master)

don, donat (give)

duc, duct (lead)

dyn, dyna, dynam (power)

ego (self)

endo (inside)

equ, equi (equal)

fer (carry)

flect (bend)

flor, flora, fleur (flower)

fract, frag (break)

fug (escape)

gastr, gastro (stomach)

gen, gene, geno (birth)

geo (earth)

List of Common Root Words (continued)

ger (old age)

gram (written)

gyn (female)

helic, helico (spiral)

heli, helio (sun)

hem, hema, hemo (blood)

herbi (plant)

hetero (other)

homeo, homo (same)

hydr, hydro (water)

imag (likeness)

iso (equal)

ject (throw)

jud, jur, just (law)

junct (join)

juven (young)

kine, kinet (motion)

lab (work)

later (side)

liber (free)

lingu (language)

loc (place)

locu, loqu (speak)

log, logo (word)

luc, lumin (light)

lun, luna, lumi (moon)

mal, male (bad)

mand (order)

mania (madness)

manu (hand)

mar, mari (sea)

mater, matr, matri (mother)

meter (measure)

migr (move)

morph (form)

mort (death)

narr (tell)

nat (born)

necr, necro (dead)

neg (no)

nom, nomin (name)

noun, nunc (declare)

numer (number)

ocu, op, opt (eye)

op, oper (work)

ortho (straight)

pale, paleo (ancient)

pater, patr, patri (father)

path (feeling)

ped, pede, pedi, pod (foot, child)

phag, phage (eat)

phil (friend, love)

phon, phono (sound)

phot, photo (light)

phys (body, nature)

pop (people)

pseud, pseudo (false)

psych, psycho (mind)

pugn, pugna (fight)

purg (clean)

pyr, pyro (fire)

rid (laugh)

rupt (burst)

scend (climb)

sci (know)

scrib, script (write)

sect (cut)

serv (keep)

sol (alone, sun)

spec, spect, spic (see)

sphere (ball)

spir (breathe)

stell (star)

techno (skill)

tel, tele, telo (far)

tele (far away)

temp, tempo (time)

term, termin (end)

ter, terr, terra (earth)

the, theo (god)

therm, thermo (heat)

urb (city)

vac (empty)

verb (word)

vid, vis (to see)

WATCHING FOR WORDS

There's no way to provide a complete list of all root words that occur in the English language, but the list provided is a great start to figuring out many ACT vocabulary word meanings. As you go through your daily life, keep an eye out for more word roots, and watch for them to reappear in other words. The more you know, the more you can figure out—and the better your vocabulary will be!

Now, let's try some exercises to put your knowledge of root word meanings to work.

Exercise 1

Using what you learned, choose the best available definition for each word.

1. genuflect
   a. to run
   b. to bend at the knee
   c. to jump
   d. to solve

2. intercept
   a. to make known
   b. to come together
   c. to seize or hold before arrival
   d. to come between

3. concede
   a. to hinder
   b. to return
   c. to display arrogance
   d. to yield or accept as true

4. carnivorous
   a. looking for danger
   b. feeding on animal flesh
   c. seeking out parties or events
   d. excitable

5. inscription
   a. enrollment
   b. the beginning
   c. the writing or dedication on something
   d. a disaster

Exercise 2

Using what you learned, fill in the correct letters to complete the word base.

1. An instrument used to measure the <u>pressure</u> of the atmosphere:

   __ __ __ __ meter

2. Marine animals that move by expelling water from a tube under

   the <u>head</u>: __ __ __ __ __ __ __ pod

3. Moving in a direction away from a <u>center</u> or axis:

__ __ __ __ __ ifugal

4. The study of the operation of <u>air</u>crafts: __ __ __ __ nautics

5. The act of <u>speaking</u> words that are to be written or transcribed:

__ __ __ __ ation

6. To make something move in a way that resembles <u>life</u>like action:

__ __ __ __ ate

7. Something done out of <u>love</u> for or goodwill toward others:

__ __ __ __ anthropy

8. To <u>cut</u> into: in __ __ __ __

9. The process of <u>learning</u>: __ __ __ __ ition

10. A particular concept or understanding of <u>beauty</u>:

__ __ __ __ __ etics

Answers

Exercise 1

1. **b.** to bend at the knee
2. **c.** to seize or hold before arrival
3. **d.** to yield or accept as true
4. **b.** feeding on animal flesh
5. **c.** the writing or dedication on something

Exercise 2

1. <u>b a r o</u> meter

2. <u>c e p h a l o</u> pod

3. <u>c e n t r</u> ifugal

4. <u>a e r o</u> nautics

5. <u>d i c t</u> ation

6. <u>a n i m</u> ate

7. <u>p h i l</u> anthropy

8. in <u>c i s e</u>

9. <u>c o g n</u> ition

10. <u>a e s t h</u> etics

3 ▶ Deconstruct and Rebuild

In Chapter 1, you learned the meanings of common prefixes and suffixes. In Chapter 2, you learned the meanings of common base words. Now, it's time to put this knowledge to use.

Let's practice before moving on to the more complex vocabulary needed to play the games in the next section of the book, and on the ACT exam.

In the following exercises, put it all together by combining base words with prefixes and suffixes to create new words.

Exercise 1

Match the word parts from column A to the word parts in column B to create words that match the definitions that follow. Some words will be used more than once.

Column A	Column B
anti	act
con	cede
de	ceed
ex	ceive
in	cept
mis	dict
non	flect
pre	mand
re	serve
un	spect

1. To keep or store; protect. _____
2. To respond or change due to a stimulus. _____
3. To go over and above. _____
4. To charge with an offense. _____
5. To keep safe; to avoid wasteful use of. _____
6. To trick; to be false. _____
7. To order or send back; to return to custody. _____
8. An idea. _____
9. Special regard or esteem. _____
10. To foretell or declare in advance. _____
11. To cause to begin; to form. _____
12. A command or principle intended as a general course of action. _____
13. To be worthy of something. _____
14. To turn aside. _____
15. To acquire or come into possession. _____
16. To ask with authority. _____

17. With the exclusion of. _____

18. To view critically or closely. _____

19. To keep back or hold. _____

20. To surpass; to go ahead or in front of. _____

Exercise 2

Match the word parts from column A to the word parts in column B to create words that match the definitions that follow. Some words will be used more than once. An asterisk (*) denotes that two entries from column B are used (don't forget to drop the silent *e* if necessary).

Column A	Column B
auto	ance
bio	ary
cardio	ate
jur	ation
kinet	ic
lumin	graph
migr	logy
narr	ous
opt	or
phon	y

1. An instrument that measures the movement of the heart.

_____

2. Emitting or reflecting light. _____

3. The act of moving from one country or region to another.

_____

*4. Of or relating to a signature. _____

5. One who is sworn to give a verdict in a dispute. _____

6. The study of living organisms. _____

7. To tell a story in detail. _____

8. Of or relating to the eye. _____

9. Of or relating to sound. _____

*10. The written story of someone's life. _____

11. The study of the heart. _____

12. A body of people who are called on to give a verdict in a dispute.

_____

13. Of or related to motion. _____

14. The state or quality of emitting or reflecting light.

_____

*15. One who tells a story in detail. _____

16. A person of prominence or brilliance. _____

17. Not genuine; false. _____

18. A signature. _____

19. The act of telling or recounting a story in detail. _____

20. To move from one country or region to another.

_____

Exercise 3

Insert definitions for the following words based on your knowledge of prefixes, suffixes, and base word meanings.

1. bibliomania: _____

2. enumerate: _____

3. vacuous: _____

4. temporal: _____

5. autobiographic: _____

6. paternally: _____

7. chromatograph: _____

8. bioavailability: _____

9. amphibious: _____

10. anthropologic: _____

Answers

Exercise 1

1. preserve
2. react
3. exceed
4. indict
5. conserve
6. deceive
7. remand
8. concept
9. respect
10. predict
11. conceive
12. precept
13. deserve
14. deflect
15. receive
16. demand
17. except
18. inspect
19. reserve
20. precede

Exercise 2

1. cardiograph
2. luminous
3. migration
*4. autographic
5. juror
6. biology
7. narrate
8. optic
9. phonic
*10. biography

11. cardiology
12. jury
13. kinetic
14. luminance
*15. narrator
16. luminary
17. phony
18. autograph
19. narration
20. migrate

Exercise 3

Answers will vary; possible answers are provided.

1. bibliomania: extreme love or passion for books
2. enumerate: to determine the number of
3. vacuous: emptied; lacking content
4. temporal: relating to time
5. autobiographic: about one's self
6. paternally: relating to a father
7. chromatograph: an instrument for analyzing color
8. bioavailability: the rate at which a substance is absorbed into an organism
9. amphibious: able to exist on land and in water
10. anthropologic: relating to study of humans

II

Build an Awesome Vocabulary . . . with Games

4 ▶ Crossword Puzzles

In this chapter, you'll put what you've learned in Part I to use with these fun vocabulary building crossword puzzles.

Instructions

Read the clues below, then solve for each by filling in the squares with letters to form ACT vocabulary words. The answers will read from left to right, or from top to bottom.

If you need help, a list containing all the words used in this chapter can be found on page 38. Scan the list to see if you can identify the word you're looking for.

If you're completely stumped, give yourself a break by turning to another game or doing something else for a while. You can always come back and finish another time.

Answers to all of the puzzles can be found at the end of the chapter, but don't peek until you've given each game your very best shot!

Crossword Puzzle #1

If you get stuck, take a look at the word list at the end of the chapter to see if you can find the word to match the definition in the clue.

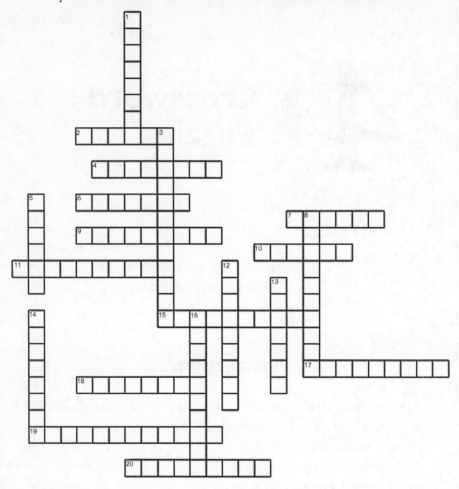

Across
2. joyous
4. merry
6. warm and friendly
7. jolly; full of good humor
9. extremely happy; euphoric
10. thrilled; overjoyed
11. carefree; sociable
15. sociable
17. friendly
18. confident; optimistic
19. lively; bubbly
20. compatible

Down
1. extremely joyful
3. thrilling
5. cheerful
8. looking for or expecting good things to happen
12. lively
13. lighthearted; high-spirited
14. agreeable
16. joyful enthusiasm

Crossword Puzzle #2

If you get stuck, take a look at the word list at the end of the chapter to see if you can find the word to match the definition in the clue.

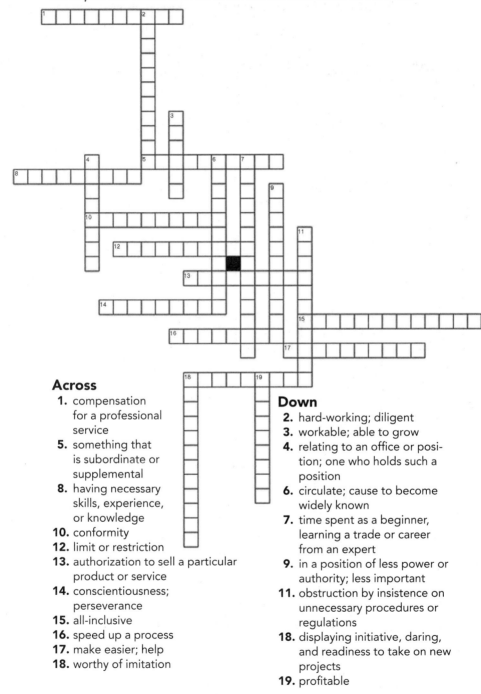

Across

1. compensation for a professional service
5. something that is subordinate or supplemental
8. having necessary skills, experience, or knowledge
10. conformity
12. limit or restriction
13. authorization to sell a particular product or service
14. conscientiousness; perseverance
15. all-inclusive
16. speed up a process
17. make easier; help
18. worthy of imitation

Down

2. hard-working; diligent
3. workable; able to grow
4. relating to an office or position; one who holds such a position
6. circulate; cause to become widely known
7. time spent as a beginner, learning a trade or career from an expert
9. in a position of less power or authority; less important
11. obstruction by insistence on unnecessary procedures or regulations
18. displaying initiative, daring, and readiness to take on new projects
19. profitable

Crossword Puzzle #3

If you get stuck, take a look at the word list at the end of the chapter to see if you can find the word to match the definition in the clue.

Across
5. active opposition or dislike
11. scathing; venomous
12. resentment or hostility; feeling of ill will
16. angry feeling of dislike or hatred
18. damaging
19. brief or direct in a way that may seem rude

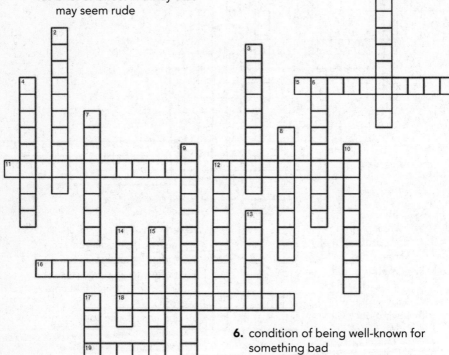

6. condition of being well-known for something bad
7. showing strong, angry feelings
8. carelessly or foolishly wasting money or time
9. deserving of strong criticism
10. someone who praises powerful people to get approval
12. unwarranted pride; superiority
13. express regret
14. long, angry speech
15. explosive
17. vengeful anger

Down
1. ill-tempered; cranky
2. blatant; conspicuous and offensive outcry
3. characterized by harsh or angry words
4. aggressively conceited and presumptuous

Crossword Puzzle #4

If you get stuck, take a look at the word list at the end of the chapter to see if you can find the word to match the definition in the clue.

Across
4. unnecessary or unwarranted
10. declaration or assertion of truth
11. of or relating to letters and letter-writing
13. enthusiastic proponent of a belief or idea; committed to a political party
14. decline; decrease
15. current holder of a particular office
17. most essential part
18. unintelligent or stupid
19. official reprimand or condemnation
20. act of being reserved or restrained; reluctant to talk or draw attention

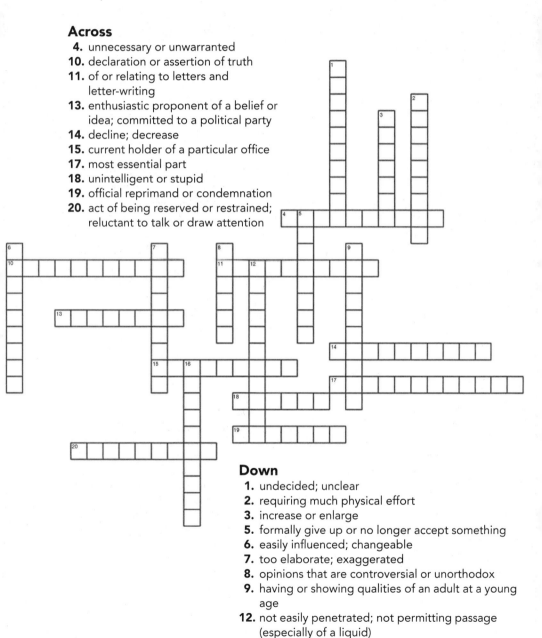

Down
1. undecided; unclear
2. requiring much physical effort
3. increase or enlarge
5. formally give up or no longer accept something
6. easily influenced; changeable
7. too elaborate; exaggerated
8. opinions that are controversial or unorthodox
9. having or showing qualities of an adult at a young age
12. not easily penetrated; not permitting passage (especially of a liquid)
16. fickle; changing on a whim

Crossword Puzzle #5

If you get stuck, take a look at the word list at the end of the chapter to see if you can find the word to match the definition in the clue.

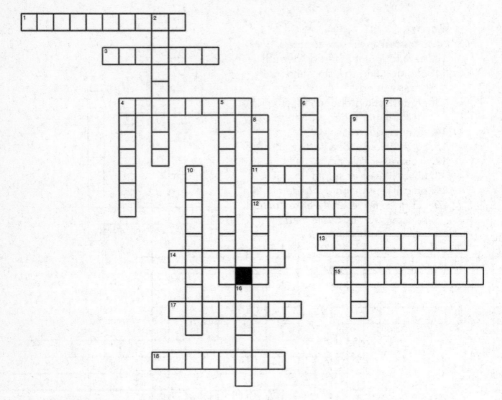

Across

1. make worse
3. lacking serious thought or intelligence
4. make lower or less important
11. wrong
12. without attention for detail; not thorough
13. placing or keeping away from people
14. sudden, disastrous collapse or downfall
15. exact copy or reproduction
17. take the place of; serve as a substitute for
18. official permission or approval

Down

2. harsh; aggressively ferocious
4. fix or correct
5. based on theory or hypothesis rather than practical knowledge
6. not straightforward; dishonest or sneaky
7. opinions that are controversial or unorthodox
8. faultless; perfect
9. quirk or unique trait
10. all alike or similar
16. excessively elaborate or showy; flowery

Crossword Puzzle #6

If you get stuck, take a look at the word list at the end of the chapter to see if you can find the word to match the definition in the clue.

Across

6. entire series or range
7. cause to do or act
8. kind; dutiful
12. excessive intolerance of opposing views
14. foreshadowing evil; foreboding
15. correct, usually in a gentle way
16. ruined the beauty or perfection of
18. impose or collect; seize

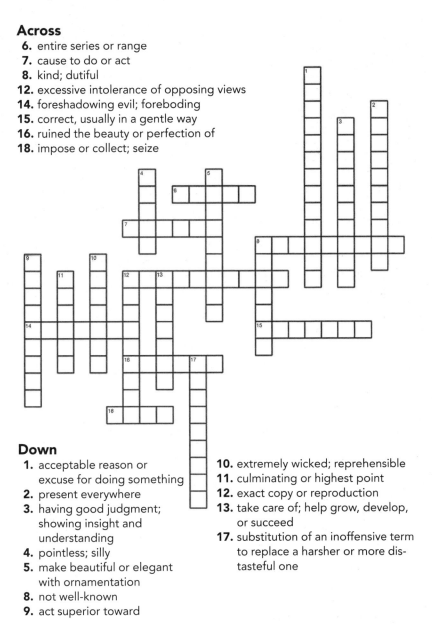

Down

1. acceptable reason or excuse for doing something
2. present everywhere
3. having good judgment; showing insight and understanding
4. pointless; silly
5. make beautiful or elegant with ornamentation
8. not well-known
9. act superior toward
10. extremely wicked; reprehensible
11. culminating or highest point
12. exact copy or reproduction
13. take care of; help grow, develop, or succeed
17. substitution of an inoffensive term to replace a harsher or more distasteful one

Crossword Puzzle #7

If you get stuck, take a look at the word list at the end of the chapter to see if you can find the word to match the definition in the clue.

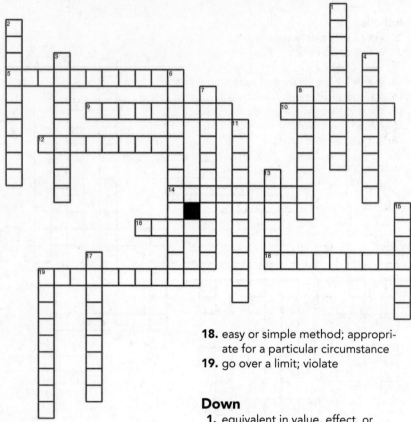

18. easy or simple method; appropriate for a particular circumstance
19. go over a limit; violate

Down
1. equivalent in value, effect, or significance
2. multicolored
3. future generations; descendents
4. swing or move back and forth
6. stealthy or secret
7. careful to consider all feelings and consequences; prudent
8. contemplate; reflect on or remember something
11. inconsistency; conflicting facts or claims
13. disprove
15. restrict; cut short
17. resourceful, clever
19. fearful

Across
5. lacking in harmony or compatibility
9. fatigue; feeling abnormal drowsiness or weariness
10. of or related to the countryside and farming
12. original work or standard used as an example for others
14. rebellious
16. shrewdness; craftiness

Crossword Puzzle #8

If you get stuck, take a look at the word list at the end of the chapter to see if you can find the word to match the definition in the clue.

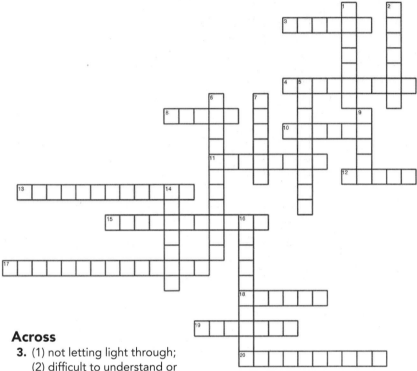

Across

3. (1) not letting light through; (2) difficult to understand or explain

4. (1) prove that someone is not guilty; (2) show that something is true

8. difficult or unpleasant circumstances; being careful, strict, or exact

10. ridicule; show contempt for

11. (1) prominent or brilliant person; (2) body that gives light

12. disregard; show scorn or contempt

13. body of voters with shared interests, identity, or goals

15. someone who tries to gain advantage through a situation

17. able to perceive small differences in similar things

18. very small in size or amount

19. dull; boring

20. including every possible element; comprehensive; complete

Down

1. confusion or disorder

2. imitate or copy

5. moral soundness

6. self-satisfaction; contentment

7. unchanging; stationary

9. capable of being bought; corrupt through bribery

14. restrict; cut short

16. willing to obey someone else

Crossword Puzzle #9

If you get stuck, take a look at the word list at the end of the chapter to see if you can find the word to match the definition in the clue.

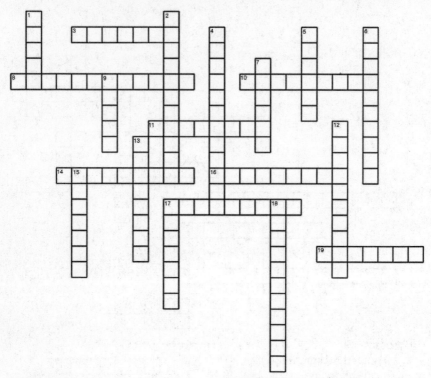

Across

3. increase or heighten
8. deceptive; pretending to be good or virtuous
10. looking for or expecting bad things to happen
11. inactive; not changing or progressing
14. accepted, done, or happening over a large area
16. similar or equivalent; showing likeness
17. unfavorable or oppositional conditions or events
19. doubtful

Down

1. rising to a great height
2. act of reducing or breaking down
4. prove the truth of something
5. motivate; provoke or stir up
6. detestable
7. humor
9. unable to move
12. harshly critical
13. state of being unconscious, unaware, or forgotten
15. take or bring back
17. give notice; tell
18. of or relating to earth or land

Crossword Puzzle #10

If you get stuck, take a look at the word list at the end of the chapter to see if you can find the word to match the definition in the clue.

Across

3. boring or dull; slow or awkward because of weight or size
6. prevent something from happening
8. kiss
10. wanting to appear more successful or important than one really is
12. clumsy or inexpert
14. misrepresent or give a false impression
15. become less strong or intense
16. unwilling; reluctant
17. abundant

Down

1. without hope
2. wheedle; coax; persuade
3. ancestor
4. easily affected or influenced
5. of or related to the sense of smell
6. large amount
7. unable to be corrected through punishment
9. remote or removed; standoffish
11. concerned with giving importance to possessions
13. wipe out

Word List for Chapter 4

abominable	censure	effervescent	guile
adversity	circumspect	elated	heinous
affable	complacency	embellish	heresy
affirmation	compliance	emulate	homogeneous
aloof	comprehensive	enhance	honorarium
ambivalent	congenial	enterprising	hypocritical
amicable	constituency	epistolary	idiosyncrasy
analogous	constraint	erroneous	impeccable
animosity	convivial	euphemism	impermeable
antagonism	cursory	exacerbate	inane
apprenticeship	curtail	exemplary	incite
apprise	debacle	exhaustive	incongruous
arrogance	degradation	exhilarating	incorrigible
augment	deride	expedient	incumbent
belie	despondent	expedite	induce
blithe	detrimental	exuberance	industrious
bombastic	devious	facilitate	inept
bucolic	diligence	facsimile	inert
bumptious	diminution	fanaticism	ingenious
buoyant	discerning	florid	insouciant
bureaucracy	discrepancy	flout	insurgent
cajole	discriminating	franchise	integrity
cantankerous	disprove	gamut	jocund
capricious	disseminate	gratuitous	jovial
censorious	dubious	gregarious	jubilant

justification	opportunist	reprehensible	terrestrial
laborious	optimistic	reprove	terse
lament	oscillate	reticence	theoretical
lethargic	osculate	retract	tirade
levity	partisan	rife	transgress
levy	patronize	rigor	tremulous
loath	pessimism	ruminate	truculent
lofty	ponderous	sanction	turmoil
lucrative	posterity	sanguine	ubiquitous
luminary	preclude	scanty	vacuous
malleable	precocious	seclusion	variegated
marred	pretentious	stagnant	vehement
materialism	prevalent	static	venal
mirthful	prodigal	submissive	viable
notoriety	profusion	subordinate	vindicate
nurture	progenitor	subside	vitriolic
obliterate	prototype	subsidiary	vituperative
oblivion	qualified	substantiate	vivacious
obscure	quintessence	supplant	vociferous
obtuse	rancor	surreptitious	volatile
official	rapturous	susceptible	wrath
officious	rectify	sycophant	zenith
olfactory	refute	tantamount	
ominous	relegate	tedious	
opaque	renounce	tenet	

Answers

Crossword Puzzle #1

Across
2. blithe
4. mirthful
6. affable
7. jovial
9. rapturous
10. elated
11. insouciant
15. gregarious
17. convivial
18. sanguine
19. effervescent
20. congenial

Down
1. jubilant
3. exhilarating
5. jocund
8. optimistic
12. vivacious
13. buoyant
14. amicable
16. exuberance

Crossword Puzzle #2

Across
1. honorarium
5. subsidiary
8. qualified
10. compliance
12. constraint
13. franchise
14. diligence
15. comprehensive
16. expedite
17. facilitate
18. exemplary

Down
2. industrious
3. viable
4. official
6. disseminate
7. apprenticeship
9. subordinate
11. bureaucracy
18. enterprising
19. lucrative

Crossword Puzzle #3

Across

5. antagonism
11. vituperative
12. animosity
16. rancor
18. detrimental
19. terse

Down

1. cantankerous
2. vociferous
3. vitriolic
4. bumptious
6. notoriety
7. vehement
8. prodigal
9. reprehensible
10. sycophant
12. arrogance
13. lament
14. tirade
15. volatile
17. wrath

Crossword Puzzle #4

Across

4. gratuitous
10. affirmation
11. epistolary
13. partisan
14. diminution
15. incumbent
17. quintessence
18. obtuse
19. censure
20. reticence

Down

1. ambivalent
2. laborious
3. augment
5. renounce
6. malleable
7. bombastic
8. tenets
9. precocious
12. impermeable
16. capricious

Crossword Puzzle #5

Across

1. exacerbate
3. vacuous
4. relegate
11. erroneous
12. cursory
13. seclusion
14. debacle
15. facsimile
17. supplant
18. sanction

Down

2. truculent
4. rectify
5. theoretical
6. devious
7. heresy
8. impeccable
9. idiosyncrasy
10. homogeneous
16. florid

Crossword Puzzle #6

Across

6. gamut
7. induce
8. officious
12. fanaticism
14. ominous
15. reprove
16. marred
18. levy

Down

1. justification
2. ubiquitous
3. discerning
4. inane
5. embellish
8. obscure
9. patronize
10. heinous
11. zenith
12. facsimile
13. nurture
17. euphemism

Crossword Puzzle #7

Across

5. incongruous
9. lethargic
10. bucolic
12. prototype
14. insurgent
16. guile
18. expedient
19. transgress

Down

1. tantamount
2. variegated
3. posterity
4. oscillate
6. surreptitious
7. circumspect
8. ruminate
11. discrepancy
13. refute
15. curtail
17. ingenious
19. tremulous

Crossword Puzzle #8

Across

3. opaque
4. vindicate
8. rigor
10. deride
11. luminary
12. flout
13. constituency
15. opportunist
17. discriminating
18. scanty
19. tedious
20. exhaustive

Down

1. turmoil
2. emulate
5. integrity
6. complacency
7. static
9. venal
14. curtail
16. submissive

Crossword Puzzle #9

Across
3. enhance
8. hypocritical
10. pessimism
11. stagnant
14. prevalent
16. analogous
17. adversity
19. dubious

Down
1. lofty
2. degradation
4. substantiate
5. incite
6. abominable
7. levity
9. inert
12. censorious
13. oblivion
15. retract
17. apprise
18. terrestrial

Crossword Puzzle #10

Across
3. ponderous
6. preclude
8. osculate
10. pretentious
12. inept
14. belie
15. subside
16. loath
17. rife

Down
1. despondent
2. cajole
3. progenitor
4. susceptible
5. olfactory
6. profusion
7. incorrigible
9. aloof
11. materialism
13. obliterate

CHAPTER

5 ▶ **Anagrams**

In this chapter, you will deconstruct ACT vocabulary words to find at least 10 new words hidden inside of each. If any of these vocabulary words are unfamiliar, be sure to look them up in the glossary at the back of the book.

Instructions

Rearrange the letters in each word below to spell as many new words as you can. Each word must be made up of a minimum of three letters—one- and two-letter words do not count. Try to find at least 10 words for each ACT vocabulary word before moving on to the next one. For an additional challenge, set a timer or stopwatch for 10 minutes. See how many words you can find before time is up!

Sample words can be found at the end of the chapter. If you're not familiar with some of the words you find in the answer key, look them up to supercharge your word power!

Anagram Puzzle #1

scrupulous

(Hint: there are at least **90** words to be made from scrupulous.)

_____   _____

_____   _____

_____   _____

_____   _____

_____   _____

_____   _____

_____   _____

_____   _____

Anagram Puzzle #2

venial

(Hint: there are at least **50** words to be made from venial.)

_____   _____

_____   _____

_____   _____

_____   _____

_____   _____

_____   _____

_____   _____

Anagram Puzzle #3

negate
(Hint: there are at least **30** words to be made from negate.)

_____   _____
_____   _____
_____   _____
_____   _____
_____   _____
_____   _____
_____   _____
_____   _____

Anagram Puzzle #4

callous
(Hint: there are at least **30** words to be made from callous.)

_____   _____
_____   _____
_____   _____
_____   _____
_____   _____
_____   _____
_____   _____
_____   _____

Anagram Puzzle #5

devious
(Hint: there are at least **40** words to be made from devious.)

_____   _____
_____   _____
_____   _____
_____   _____
_____   _____
_____   _____
_____   _____
_____   _____

Anagram Puzzle #6

marred
(Hint: there are at least **30** words to be made from marred.)

_____   _____
_____   _____
_____   _____
_____   _____
_____   _____
_____   _____
_____   _____
_____   _____

Anagram Puzzle #7

verbose

(Hint: there are at least **40** words to be made from verbose.)

_____   _____

_____   _____

_____   _____

_____   _____

_____   _____

_____   _____

_____   _____

_____   _____

Anagram Puzzle #8

lavish

(Hint: there are at least **25** words to be made from lavish.)

_____   _____

_____   _____

_____   _____

_____   _____

_____   _____

_____   _____

_____   _____

Anagram Puzzle #9

notoriety
(Hint: there are at least **100** words to be made from notoriety.)

_____   _____
_____   _____
_____   _____
_____   _____
_____   _____
_____   _____
_____   _____
_____   _____

Anagram Puzzle #10

laconic
(Hint: there are at least **40** words to be made from laconic.)

_____   _____
_____   _____
_____   _____
_____   _____
_____   _____
_____   _____
_____   _____

Answers

Anagram Puzzle #1

clop	curs	pul	sop
clops	cusp	puls	sops
col	cusps	purl	sorus
cols	cuss	purls	sou
cop	locus	pus	soul
cops	lop	puss	souls
cor	lops	roc	soup
corps	loss	rocs	soups
corpus	loup	roup	sour
cors	loups	roups	sours
coup	lour	scop	sous
coups	lupus	scops	spur
crop	oculus	scour	spurs
crops	ops	scours	sulcus
cross	opus	scup	sup
croup	ors	scups	sups
croups	our	slop	surplus
cru	ours	slops	upcurl
crus	plus	slur	upcurls
cup	pol	slurp	ups
cuprous	pols	slurps	urus
cups	pour	slurs	usurp
cur	pours	sol	usurps
curl	pro	sols	
curls	pros	solus	

Anagram Puzzle #2

ail	lain	liven	veil
ain	lane	nail	vein
ale	lav	naive	veinal
alevin	lave	nave	vela
alien	lea	navel	vena
alive	lean	nevi	venal
ane	lei	nil	venial
ani	lev	vail	via
anile	levin	vain	vial
anvil	liane	vale	vie
ave	lie	valine	vile
élan	lien	van	vina
evil	line	vane	vinal
ilea	live	veal	vine

Anagram Puzzle #3

age	eng	gent	tae
agene	eta	get	tag
agent	gan	geta	tan
ane	gat	gnat	tang
ant	gate	nag	tea
ante	gee	neat	tee
ate	gen	nee	teen
eat	gene	neg	ten
eaten	genet	net	tenge

Anagram Puzzle #4

all	cauls	culls	sac
alls	coal	lac	sal
also	coals	local	salol
call	col	locals	scull
calls	cola	locus	sol
callus	colas	oca	sou
calo	cols	olla	soul
caul	cull	ollas	

Anagram Puzzle #5

dev	doves	ouds	vids
die	due	side	vie
dies	dues	sod	vied
dis	dui	sou	vies
dive	duo	sue	vis
dives	duos	sued	vise
doe	eds	use	vised
does	ides	used	void
dos	ids	vid	voids
dose	ode	vide	
douse	odes	video	
dove	oud	videos	

Anagram Puzzle #6

are	derm	mad	ram
arm	derma	made	rare
armed	dram	mae	read
dam	dream	mar	ream
dame	drear	mare	rear
dare	ear	mead	rearm
darer	era	med	red
dear	err	rad	rem

Anagram Puzzle #7

bee	ever	rob	sever
beer	eves	robe	sob
beers	obese	robes	sober
bees	obverse	robs	soever
bore	orb	roe	sorb
bores	orbs	roes	sore
breve	ore	rose	vee
breves	ores	rove	veer
bro	ors	roves	veers
bros	over	see	vees
brose	reb	seer	verb
ere	rebs	ser	verbs
eros	res	sere	verse
erose	rev	serve	verso
eve	revs	servo	

Anagram Puzzle #8

ahi	hails	sal	via
ahis	has	shiv	vial
ahs	his	silva	vials
ail	lash	vail	vis
ails	lav	vails	visa
ash	lavs	vas	
hail	sail		

Anagram Puzzle #9

enroot	ono	tier	tot
entity	onto	tin	tote
entry	ore	tine	toter
eon	orient	tint	toy
inert	ort	tinter	toyer
inro	otter	tiny	toyon
inter	otto	tire	trey
into	rein	tiro	trine
intro	rent	tit	trio
ion	ret	titer	trite
ire	retint	titre	triton
iron	riot	toe	tritone
irony	rite	ton	trot
net	roe	tone	troy
nit	root	toner	try
nite	rooty	tonier	tyer
niter	rot	tony	tyin
nitery	rote	too	tyre
nitre	roti	toon	tyro
nitro	roto	toot	yen
nitty	rotten	tooter	yet
noir	rye	tor	yeti
nor	ten	tore	yin
nori	tenor	tori	yon
not	tent	torn	yoni
note	tern	tort	yore
noter	tetri	torte	
one	tie	tortoni	

Anagram Puzzle #10

ail	clonic	conical	loan
ain	coal	icon	loci
alnico	coca	ion	loin
aloin	coil	lac	nail
ani	coin	laic	nil
calico	col	lain	noil
calo	cola	lin	oca
can	colic	linac	oil
ciao	con	lino	oilcan
clan	conic	lion	

6 ▶ Acrostics

In this chapter, you will use your knowledge of an ACT vocabulary word's meaning to create a fun acrostic poem. This activity will also help you remember the spelling of each vocabulary word by breaking it down to create a poem.

Instructions

An acrostic poem begins with a word as its subject. The word is written vertically from top to bottom, and each line of the poem begins with a different letter from the subject word. Although you can make this poem rhyme if you like, rhyming is not necessary in an acrostic. In fact, lines could be made up of just one word.

The following is an example of an acrostic using the word **school**:

S tudying hard in each of our subjects
C lasses can be easy or hard, fun, or tedious
H ow will we get all this homework done?
O ur teachers guide us through lectures and assignments
O ften we wait until the last minute to cram
L earning what we need to know for the future

Notice that each line in the acrostic has something to do with the subject word, **school**. When completing the following acrostics, make sure that each line refers back to the subject word. This will help you to remember its meaning when you're taking the ACT exam.

There are no right or wrong answers for this game, so be as clever, creative, or outlandish as you like. Write whatever helps you remember the definition the best—and have fun!

Acrostic #1: SINUOUS

Something that is **sinuous** curves in and out and winds or bends. (Example: The stream took a *sinuous* path through the woods.)

S _____
I _____
N _____
U _____
O _____
U _____
S _____

Acrostic #2: VILIFY

To **vilify** is to say or write harsh, critical things about someone. (Example: The opposition did not just disagree with the politician; they tried to *vilify* him in the media.)

V _____
I _____
L _____
I _____
F _____
Y _____

Acrostic #3: LOATHE

To **loathe** is to show great dislike or disgust.
(Example: He could tell from the look on my face when he served it that I *loathe* broccoli.)

L _____
O _____
A _____
T _____
H _____
E _____

Acrostic #4: BLATANT

Something that is **blatant** is obvious.
(Example: I didn't mind that she was late; what bothered me was that her excuse was a *blatant* lie.)

B _____
L _____
A _____
T _____
A _____
N _____
T _____

Acrostic #5: APATHY

Apathy is a lack of energy or interest.
(Example: Her *apathy* toward sports is a direct result of having to sit through endless football games when she was younger.)

A _____
P _____
A _____
T _____
H _____
Y _____

Acrostic #6: DEVISE

To **devise** is to invent or create something.
(Example: He's hard to deceive, so we'll have to *devise* a plan to get him to the surprise party.)

D _____
E _____
V _____
I _____
S _____
E _____

Acrostic #7: EXALT

To **exalt** is to glorify or praise someone or something.
(Example: She always goes out of her way to *exalt* the flavor of a home-made meal.)

E _____

X _____

A _____

L _____

T _____

Acrostic #8: PALPABLE

Something that is **palpable** can be easily perceived or felt.
(Example: When her rival walked into the room, the tension was *palpable*.)

P _____

A _____

L _____

P _____

A _____

B _____

L _____

E _____

Acrostic #9: IMPEDE

To **impede** is to hinder or get in the way.
(Example: Lack of strong leadership will really *impede* our progress with this project.)

I _____
M _____
P _____
E _____
D _____
E _____

Acrostic #10: FERVOR

Fervor refers to extreme ardor or excitement.
(Example: The crowd clapped politely for the opening act, but worked themselves up to a *fervor* when the star stepped out on stage.)

F _____
E _____
R _____
V _____
O _____
R _____

Answers

Answers in this chapter will vary; a sample answer is below.

Acrostic #1:

S	snakelike and winding
I	indirect and meandering
N	naturally curving
U	undulating
O	openly circuitous
U	upwardly winding
S	slowly spiraling

Jumbles

In this chapter, you will learn to spell ACT words by rearranging the letters to discover vocabulary words. You should find it easier to remember the definitions of these words because they are linked by common subjects.

Instructions

Unscramble the words in each jumble by placing one letter in each box to spell ACT vocabulary words.

If you need help, a list containing all the ACT words used in this book can be found on page 137. Scan the list to see if you can identify the word(s) you're looking for. If you're completely stumped, give yourself a break by turning to another game or doing something else for a while. You can always come back and finish at another time.

Answers to all of the puzzles can be found at the end of the chapter, but don't peek until you've given each game your very best shot!

Jumble #1: Cold, Hard Cash

This jumble is made up of words that are used when talking about money—saving, spending, or even wasting.

FLAGTYIRU ☐☐☐☐☐☐☐☐☐

SERMILY ☐☐☐☐☐☐☐

CETIPANT ☐☐☐☐☐☐☐☐

TRESYPPRIO ☐☐☐☐☐☐☐☐☐☐

QANUREDS ☐☐☐☐☐☐☐☐

CUSPEIOUNIM ☐☐☐☐☐☐☐☐☐☐☐

Jumble #2: Let's Get Along

This jumble is made up of words that can be used when trying to make the best of a situation.

COYCILANITRO ☐☐☐☐☐☐☐☐☐☐☐☐

PEAPEAS ☐☐☐☐☐☐☐

FEERENCED ☐☐☐☐☐☐☐☐☐

RATIOELAME ☐☐☐☐☐☐☐☐☐☐

ENSONSUSC ☐☐☐☐☐☐☐☐☐

LEORECINC ☐☐☐☐☐☐☐☐☐

Jumble #3: Nighty-Night

The words in this game are ones you'd hear in the evening or night-time hours.

ARCTLEGIH   ☐☐☐☐☐☐☐☐☐

ULAOCTNNR   ☐☐☐☐☐☐☐☐☐

ACOLHYN   ☐☐☐☐☐☐☐

EOSPER   ☐☐☐☐☐☐

ALQRIUTN   ☐☐☐☐☐☐☐☐

ENWA   ☐☐☐☐

Jumble #4: Past Tense

These words describe things that are going . . . going . . . gone.

CACHIRA   ☐☐☐☐☐☐☐

OETSOELB   ☐☐☐☐☐☐☐☐

ONSCMNARHAI   ☐☐☐☐☐☐☐☐☐☐☐

EIVRMALP   ☐☐☐☐☐☐☐☐

IGSEETV   ☐☐☐☐☐☐☐

TRAFICTA   ☐☐☐☐☐☐☐☐

Jumble #5: Know-It-All

These words describe those who are recognized for being wise.

AOGCUSSAI   ☐☐☐☐☐☐☐☐☐

MNENTEI   ☐☐☐☐☐☐☐

AYRMINUL   ☐☐☐☐☐☐☐☐

ASENTPI   ☐☐☐☐☐☐☐

PPSRIOSCUCIAE   ☐☐☐☐☐☐☐☐☐☐☐☐☐

BERELAVNE   ☐☐☐☐☐☐☐☐☐

Jumble #6: Mangia!

This game comprises words that you might hear when talking about eating and drinking.

MIEIBB   ☐☐☐☐☐☐

SLUTOGUONT   ☐☐☐☐☐☐☐☐☐☐

IULOBUBS   ☐☐☐☐☐☐☐☐

AMFISH   ☐☐☐☐☐☐

AGONFRIG   ☐☐☐☐☐☐☐☐

TESOABUSMI   ☐☐☐☐☐☐☐☐☐☐

Jumble #7: Enough Already!

You might use these words to describe something that's over the top.

SOBABITCM ☐☐☐☐☐☐☐☐

IEFFVUES ☐☐☐☐☐☐☐

NOEASIDRG ☐☐☐☐☐☐☐☐

NOTUTTIESASO ☐☐☐☐☐☐☐☐☐☐☐

LIDROF ☐☐☐☐☐☐

SESRULUOFPU ☐☐☐☐☐☐☐☐☐☐

Jumble #8: Too Cool for School

The answers below are words you might hear while you're in the classroom.

DICTIACD ☐☐☐☐☐☐☐☐

DIEMRELA ☐☐☐☐☐☐☐☐

RUDEITE ☐☐☐☐☐☐☐

METO ☐☐☐☐

BIRDAGE ☐☐☐☐☐☐☐

REELCARB ☐☐☐☐☐☐☐☐

Jumble #9: Puttin' on the Ritz

When you're showing how sophisticated you are, you might use these words.

OLOOTMAPNICS ⬜⬜⬜⬜⬜⬜⬜⬜⬜⬜⬜⬜

EELIT ⬜⬜⬜⬜⬜

ETELNEG ⬜⬜⬜⬜⬜⬜⬜

SLABE ⬜⬜⬜⬜⬜

COURDEM ⬜⬜⬜⬜⬜⬜

SPURETENTIO ⬜⬜⬜⬜⬜⬜⬜⬜⬜⬜⬜

Jumble #10: Don't Be That Person

You wouldn't want the words in this jumble used to describe you!

BGTRAGAR   ☐☐☐☐☐☐☐

QUBURES   ☐☐☐☐☐☐

RUSHLICH   ☐☐☐☐☐☐☐

RETES   ☐☐☐☐☐

RUNCUTLET   ☐☐☐☐☐☐☐☐

MENUTIPD   ☐☐☐☐☐☐☐

Answers

Jumble #1: Cold, Hard Cash
FLAGTYIRU	**FRUGALITY**
SERMILY	**MISERLY**
CETIPANT	**PITTANCE**
TRESYPPRIO	**PROSPERITY**
QANUREDS	**SQUANDER**
CUSPEIOUNIM	**IMPECUNIOUS**

Jumble #2: Can't We All Just Get Along?
COYCILANITRO	**CONCILIATORY**
PEAPEAS	**APPEASE**
FEERENCED	**DEFERENCE**
RATIOELAME	**AMELIORATE**
ENSONSUSC	**CONSENSUS**
LEORECINC	**RECONCILE**

Jumble #3: Nighty-Night
ARCTLEGIH	**LETHARGIC**
ULAOCTNNR	**NOCTURNAL**
ACOLHYN	**HALCYON**
EOSPER	**REPOSE**
ALQRIUTN	**TRANQUIL**
ENWA	**WANE**

Jumble #4: Past Tense
CACHIRA	**ARCHAIC**
OETSOELB	**OBSOLETE**
ONSCMNARHAI	**ANACHRONISM**
EIVRMALP	**PRIMEVAL**
IGSEETV	**VESTIGE**
TRAFICTA	**ARTIFACT**

Jumble #5: Know-It-All

A O G C U S S A I	**SAGACIOUS**
M N E N T E I	**EMINENT**
A Y R M I N U L	**LUMINARY**
A S E N T P I	**SAPIENT**
P P S R I O S C U C I A E	**PERSPICACIOUS**
B E R E L A V N E	**VENERABLE**

Jumble #6: Mangia!

M I E I B B	**IMBIBE**
S L U T O G U O N T	**GLUTTONOUS**
I U L O B U B S	**BIBULOUS**
A M F I S H	**FAMISH**
A G O N F R I G	**FORAGING**
T E S O A B U S M I	**ABSTEMIOUS**

Jumble #7: Enough Already!

S O B A B I T C M	**BOMBASTIC**
I E F F V U E S	**EFFUSIVE**
N O E A S I D R G	**GRANDIOSE**
N O T U T T I E S A S O	**OSTENTATIOUS**
L I D R O F	**FLORID**
S E S R U L U O F P U	**SUPERFLUOUS**

Jumble #8: Too Cool for School

D I C T I A C D	**DIDACTIC**
D I E M R E L A	**REMEDIAL**
R U D E I T E	**ERUDITE**
M E T O	**TOME**
B I R D A G E	**ABRIDGE**
R E E L C A R B	**CEREBRAL**

Jumble #9: Puttin' on the Ritz

OLOOTMAPNICS	**COSMOPOLITAN**
EELIT	**ELITE**
ETELNEG	**GENTEEL**
SLABE	**BLASE**
COURDEM	**DECORUM**
SPURETENTIO	**PRETENTIOUS**

Jumble #10: Don't Be That Guy

BGTRAGAR	**BRAGGART**
QUBURES	**BRUSQUE**
RUSHLICH	**CHURLISH**
RETES	**TERSE**
RUNCUTLET	**TRUCULENT**
MENUTIPD	**IMPUDENT**

8

▶ **Word Searches**

In this chapter, you will reinforce your ability to recognize ACT vocabulary words by finding them in the following word search puzzles.

Instructions

Each word on the right side of the game is hidden somewhere within the letters on the left side. Words will be found exactly as they are spelled, but may be written left to right, right to left, up and down, or diagonally.

Answers are found at the end of the chapter. Be sure to look up any unfamiliar words in the glossary at the back of the book, because it's not enough to know how the words are spelled—you will need to know their meanings, as well, when you take the ACT exam!

Word Search Game #1

```
S A I E L B A T C A R T N C Y
D L F E M O S N I W L C A R D
U J R N Q H Z P K C T H H I I
Y G Y K M U U K H C W I X T F
W W A O T M Z Q K X B C G E R
W K D R X U J B P N P A A R E
B C E E R L K U D S X N G I P
G P L Y W U J M X F C E C O U
L R T I L U L A O X I R U N D
T A N O M A L O U S C Y I U W
I B R F P M U J U H J N C T O
W I R N B C Y T Z S V S B L Z
Q M D C N G H C I T E M R E H
D L O M U N D A N E X R W M R
Y D P A B D I C A T E K K W C
```

CHICANERY
TRACTABLE
GARRULOUS
ABDICATE
WINSOME
MUNDANE
PERFIDY
HERMETIC
ANOMALOUS
CRITERION

Word Search Game #2

```
A X A B F F D F Y V D E Q W S
S T G T V Q C Z E G I J J M T
C A P W N G Z M A G P V A S S
V L H T V E S T I G E S W C I
L L R K E E G U L E R K X H N
D E N O U N C E T S T Q Q R O
M V D H Q H C T K U N Q H M D
S I Z F S V O A S Q I K S S E
A A J N U D H R H S I M A F H
D T T F R L E U J T X A G L B
S E V D B K S T U Q J F Q I Y
E I Y C N X I A D V S Z J O C
L G I Y J V V S Y K G R J S H
J R N U V U E V T F V L W E U
N S M P E D O G M A T I C B I
```

DENOUNCE
ALLEVIATE
BRUSQUE
SATURATE
VESTIGE
INTREPID
FAMISH
HEDONIST
COHESIVE
DOGMATIC

Word Search Game #3

```
N  N  I  J  L  Z  Q  A  H  G  C  S  D  F  C
K  S  P  N  B  X  Z  N  O  Q  W  C  Z  A  E
V  N  Y  T  I  C  I  L  P  U  D  H  K  N  S
E  R  O  B  T  J  Y  Y  V  A  P  I  D  G  S
P  B  K  F  Q  T  H  E  I  U  K  S  Z  I  X
U  S  D  I  B  H  M  S  M  U  V  M  C  N  X
Z  T  N  L  N  D  R  U  T  C  A  D  D  E  C
W  L  E  Z  Z  C  E  R  C  J  B  Z  T  B  S
P  Q  A  N  V  I  I  T  A  J  J  A  L  D  X
M  X  U  N  A  M  I  S  X  X  T  U  A  I  N
W  F  D  P  G  C  O  B  I  N  M  C  I  Q  G
E  L  V  B  B  U  I  A  E  V  P  M  V  F  Z
M  H  H  P  F  Z  I  T  X  A  E  X  O  Z  F
P  Y  K  E  P  A  O  D  Y  Y  Q  Q  J  X  N
E  A  O  O  N  P  E  S  T  N  V  Y  N  N  Y
```

SCHISM
TENACITY
VAPID
POTENTATE
JOVIAL
ABSTRUSE
INCISIVE
BENIGN
LANGUID
DUPLICITY

Word Search Game #4

```
J  B  Z  D  F  A  J  L  E  Y  W  F  X  T  G
R  L  Z  O  E  N  R  R  O  B  J  T  D  J  E
D  S  M  E  S  I  E  C  U  P  C  J  E  J  O
X  X  A  N  M  Y  F  G  N  I  R  P  C  B  H
G  Q  L  G  W  O  X  I  T  T  P  P  O  B  D
B  N  I  J  A  F  T  O  S  P  O  L  R  M  X
Y  W  C  M  D  C  X  I  U  S  I  L  U  P  Y
F  K  I  B  M  I  I  F  P  H  O  P  M  A  D
I  N  O  Y  U  L  R  O  T  E  B  V  P  N  L
W  A  U  Q  U  E  H  H  U  X  O  S  W  A  U
W  V  S  J  B  E  V  K  Q  S  Q  S  Z  C  R
V  E  O  Z  T  N  T  N  E  C  S  A  N  E  V
C  R  H  P  U  H  X  H  S  F  V  V  B  A  G
B  Y  A  V  X  O  Q  S  R  Z  I  Q  M  C  I
C  I  F  I  L  O  R  P  S  W  K  U  F  U  R
```

KNAVERY
PROLIFIC
OSSIFIED
SAGACIOUS
NASCENT
QUIXOTIC
PANACEA
DECORUM
MALICIOUS
EPITOME

Word Search Game #5

```
B S K D H S I L R U H C Z S B
S Z E W P Z E S U L C E R N F
T W X Y A X U E M J W Y I Q T
T A V S I N Q Q Q G Y I F X R
Z W F C P D T J I T O H L K L
Y K O Q V A Q O I U N D Z Q T
F N I K C L V V N U Z M O E B
C I B R E C A Z A Z Y B M G S
X R P L X R H W D I Q P B R Y
T O P L P A B C I Y B D S E F
U K G E C X S R P Y T O V S L
I B D D O Y B P I V L I I S Q
X R D Y N O M I S R A P M M K
C I P S Z K S S N M M G Z N H
B G N O L Z A Y I S Q U I L E
```

EGRESS
DEPRAVITY
PARSIMONY
RECLUSE
ACERBIC
ENMITY
INSIPID
CHURLISH
LEXICON
WANTON

Word Search Game #6

```
E D Q Y P C L V B I K N X M P
V M N E W E Y B R I G A N D T
O S E R V I L E A L L C U U N
Z W B I B F Z F N D N H N C A
M O S N T O L E M O R S C X D
L Y C O H N J E N J H H P Z R
S A L I E N T N W E G A Q F O
W J T R O P P A R G D B Z R C
V Z J U N U A N A R C H Y N S
D L B G D G G I H S L D T C I
Z N C S U O R E F I C O V P D
A B E A D V E R S A R Y Z D F
F L Q P E C N E L U P O K L R
U C I D P G S G U P W P H G T
X X U A W Z Q W T N P D G F N
```

VOCIFEROUS
OPULENCE
SALIENT
ADVERSARY
WIZENED
BRIGAND
RAPPORT
ANARCHY
DISCORDANT
SERVILE

Word Search Game #7

```
O  L  E  S  O  T  E  R  I  C  I  Q  V  L  G
G  O  M  C  O  Y  E  D  U  T  I  P  R  U  T
R  C  L  M  N  T  N  E  V  L  O  S  Y  O  Q
Y  Z  Z  S  Y  G  N  T  N  I  B  R  I  C  T
K  B  V  V  J  C  U  S  A  E  A  L  A  X  L
R  T  V  Y  O  H  I  L  N  D  G  O  U  A  T
R  P  V  K  T  X  T  R  N  O  M  Y  R  Z  E
L  X  Z  V  O  R  L  A  R  N  L  E  W  R  H
T  S  T  H  U  P  U  B  C  A  M  I  E  T  Z
U  S  N  I  S  Q  M  A  Y  E  C  T  A  T  H
A  G  S  G  Z  I  P  X  H  B  S  J  L  J  G
F  M  Y  I  N  F  W  P  X  U  U  B  O  I  H
R  U  Z  S  W  E  E  H  A  M  F  I  T  H  X
S  E  D  S  U  O  I  D  I  T  S  A  F  I  Q
S  R  L  X  X  P  A  Q  E  S  O  R  O  M  I
```

ESOTERIC
IMBROGLIO
QUANDARY
MOROSE
FASTIDIOUS
TURPITUDE
AUSTERE
SOLVENT
ALTRUISM
EPHEMERAL

Word Search Game #8

```
H  Q  P  O  G  A  F  Q  C  T  M  S  J  I  F
M  K  C  S  H  G  B  V  H  Q  G  X  R  M  T
Z  H  U  Y  X  I  E  T  Y  H  P  O  E  N  Y
F  G  X  N  Z  M  N  B  X  I  V  N  Z  H  R
B  H  C  D  S  U  J  O  E  T  I  D  U  R  E
C  F  W  I  L  O  Z  C  C  S  X  E  N  B  B
E  O  U  C  A  E  P  U  W  U  K  T  U  X  F
T  X  X  H  T  T  T  L  H  I  L  S  J  R  G
A  U  A  O  Y  D  C  A  J  R  K  A  X  K  S
G  A  F  T  T  M  O  R  N  G  G  C  T  U  U
I  U  Z  O  W  F  R  O  N  I  F  T  V  E  Z
T  T  W  M  W  E  D  U  H  J  T  G  V  E  Y
I  V  O  Y  I  A  I  T  X  W  W  S  G  O  C
M  E  R  U  J  B  A  V  U  K  C  P  B  L  B
N  R  V  L  Z  O  L  Y  A  N  G  Z  E  O  J
```

INOCULATE
MITIGATE
OCULAR
NEOPHYTE
ERUDITE
CORDIAL
ABJURE
CASTE
DICHOTOMY
OBSTINATE

Word Search Game #9

```
Y J C L S C O T A Z B V G U H
N J D Y T I R A P S I D L G O
A B G C W G Z Y C G S I I D R
L U X U Y U Q Q P O D R Z E G
Y M Y J J O B G S Q E M A O Z
S G E Z D Y F L X T Y K X Q T
D I P I X P Z G A W X B F I A
M N O C O E R C I O N U C L R
W U W E H U I G R P R I Q H C
S N W U R R C S V T L B V T H
D D H U T K Y A I P C H H L A
P A B N F G D V X J P X G M I
P T I G S B E E H T I L O V C
Y E K K D N E J W M O H J Y D
G C D L M I S E R L Y J L D B
```

ODIOUS
LITHE
INUNDATE
FURTIVE
EXPLICIT
MISERLY
INTRICATE
DISPARITY
ARCHAIC
COERCION

Word Search Game #10

```
B D Q B T C X Z M M S T O H Z
E T N B W Z P V C H R O F E V
D W T I H C D F N A V H P I B
L C T C A Z X W V E U H J Q Q
A L P R F D O E U G Y K O V O
M L C F A F S B R R K B U W Q
X P G Q H T R I Q E J G G G M
C D S T Y A C A D I U M T M O
M E Q K G R F A M G I N E N M
Q L L G Y K G A F T O S I X X
E Y A P D N M R T G I I X I O
S R T B J H I N D R A N C E T
T I X C U A J C L J L P U D V
C B H Q C I L O I R T I V C P
O J N F V I W A N E C D O T E
```

VITRIOLIC
HINDRANCE
DISDAIN
BEDLAM
ZEPHYR
TRAVESTY
CRYPTIC
ANECDOTE
ENIGMA
BRAGGART

Answers

Word Search Game #1

```
S  A  I  E  L  B  A  T  C  A  R  T  N  C  Y
D  L  F  E  M  O  S  N  I  W  L  C  A  R  D
U  J  R  N  Q  H  Z  P  K  C  T  H  H  I  I
Y  G  Y  K  M  U  U  K  H  C  W  I  X  T  F
W  W  A  O  T  M  Z  Q  K  X  B  C  G  E  R
W  K  D  R  X  U  J  B  P  N  P  A  A  R  E
B  C  E  E  R  L  K  U  D  S  X  N  G  I  P
G  P  L  Y  W  U  J  M  X  F  C  E  C  O  U
L  R  T  I  L  U  A  O  X  I  R  U  N  D
T  A  N  O  M  A  L  O  U  S  C  Y  I  U  W
I  B  R  F  P  M  U  J  U  H  J  N  C  T  O
W  I  R  N  B  C  Y  T  Z  S  V  S  B  L  Z
Q  M  D  C  N  G  H  C  I  T  E  M  R  E  H
D  L  O  M  U  N  D  A  N  E  X  R  W  M  R
Y  D  P  A  B  D  I  C  A  T  E  K  K  W  C
```

CHICANERY
TRACTABLE
GARRULOUS
ABDICATE
WINSOME
MUNDANE
PERFIDY
HERMETIC
ANOMALOUS
CRITERION

Word Search Game #2

```
A  X  A  B  F  F  D  F  Y  V  D  E  Q  W  S
S  T  G  T  V  Q  C  Z  E  G  I  J  J  M  T
C  A  P  W  N  G  Z  M  A  G  P  V  A  S  S
V  L  H  T  V  E  S  T  I  G  E  S  W  C  I
L  L  R  K  E  E  G  U  L  E  R  K  X  H  N
D  E  N  O  U  N  C  E  T  S  T  Q  Q  R  O
M  V  D  H  Q  H  C  T  K  U  N  Q  H  M  D
S  I  Z  F  S  V  O  A  S  Q  I  K  S  S  E
A  A  J  N  U  D  H  R  H  S  I  M  A  F  H
D  T  T  F  R  L  E  U  J  T  X  A  G  L  B
S  E  V  D  B  K  S  T  U  Q  J  F  Q  I  Y
E  I  Y  C  N  X  I  A  D  V  S  Z  J  O  C
L  G  I  Y  J  V  V  S  Y  K  G  R  J  S  H
J  R  N  U  V  U  E  V  T  F  V  L  W  E  U
N  S  M  P  E  D  O  G  M  A  T  I  C  B  I
```

DENOUNCE
ALLEVIATE
BRUSQUE
SATURATE
VESTIGE
INTREPID
FAMISH
HEDONIST
COHESIVE
DOGMATIC

Word Search Game #3

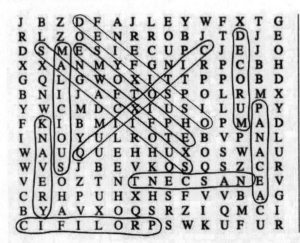

```
N  N  I  J  L  Z  Q  A  H  G  C  S  D  F  C
K  S  P  N  B  X  Z  N  O  Q  W  C  Z  A  E
V  N  Y  T  I  C  I  L  P  U  D  H  K  N  S
E  R  O  B  T  J  Y  Y  V  A  P  I  D  G  S
P  B  K  F  Q  T  H  E  I  U  K  S  Z  I  X
U  S  D  I  B  H  M  S  M  U  V  M  C  N  X
Z  T  N  L  N  D  R  U  T  C  A  D  D  E  C
W  L  E  Z  Z  C  E  R  C  J  B  Z  T  B  S
P  Q  A  N  V  I  I  T  A  J  J  A  L  D  X
M  X  U  N  A  M  I  S  X  X  T  U  A  I  N
W  F  D  P  G  C  O  B  I  N  M  C  I  Q  G
E  L  V  B  B  U  I  A  E  V  P  M  V  F  Z
M  H  H  P  F  Z  I  T  X  A  E  X  O  Z  F
P  Y  K  E  P  A  O  D  Y  Y  Q  Q  J  X  N
E  A  O  O  N  P  E  S  T  N  V  Y  N  N  Y
```

SCHISM
TENACITY
VAPID
POTENTATE
JOVIAL
ABSTRUSE
INCISIVE
BENIGN
LANGUID
DUPLICITY

Word Search Game #4

```
J  B  Z  D  F  A  J  L  E  Y  W  F  X  T  G
R  L  Z  O  E  N  R  R  O  B  J  T  D  J  E
D  S  M  E  S  I  E  C  U  P  C  J  E  J  O
X  X  A  N  M  Y  F  G  N  I  R  P  C  B  H
G  Q  L  G  W  O  X  I  T  T  P  P  O  B  D
B  N  I  J  A  F  T  O  S  P  O  L  R  M  X
Y  W  C  M  D  C  X  I  U  S  I  L  U  P  Y
F  K  I  B  M  I  F  P  H  O  P  M  A  A  D
I  N  O  Y  U  L  R  O  T  E  B  V  P  N  L
W  A  U  Q  U  E  H  H  U  X  O  S  W  A  U
W  V  S  J  B  E  V  K  O  S  Q  S  Z  C  R
V  E  O  Z  T  N  T  N  E  C  S  A  N  E  V
C  R  H  P  U  H  X  H  S  F  V  V  B  A  G
B  Y  A  V  X  O  Q  S  R  Z  I  Q  M  C  I
C  I  F  I  L  O  R  P  S  W  K  U  F  U  R
```

KNAVERY
PROLIFIC
OSSIFIED
SAGACIOUS
NASCENT
QUIXOTIC
PANACEA
DECORUM
MALICIOUS
EPITOME

Word Search Game #5

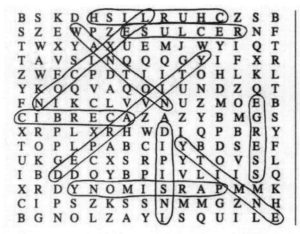

B S K D H S I L R U H C Z S B
S Z E W P Z E S U L C E R N F
T W X Y A X U E M J W Y I Q T
T A V S I N Q Q Q G Y I F X R
Z W F C P D T I I T O H L K L
Y K O Q V A Q O I U N D Z Q T
F N I K C L V N U Z M O E B
C I B R E C A Z A Z Y B M G S
X R P L X R H W D I Q P B R Y
T O P L P A B C I Y B D S E F
U K G E C X S R P Y T O V S L
I B D D O Y B P I V L I I S Q
X R D Y N O M I S R A P M M K
C I P S Z K S S N M M G Z N H
B G N O L Z A Y U S Q U I L E

EGRESS
DEPRAVITY
PARSIMONY
RECLUSE
ACERBIC
ENMITY
INSIPID
CHURLISH
LEXICON
WANTON

Word Search Game #6

E D Q Y P C L V B I K N X M P
V M N E W E Y B R I G A N D T
O S E R V I L E A L L C U U N
Z W B I B F Z F N D N H N C A
M O S N T O L E M O R S C X D
L Y C O H N J E N I H H P Z R
S A L I E N T N W E G A Q F O
W J T R O P P A R G D B Z R C
V Z J U N U A N A R C H Y N S
D L B G D G G I H S L D T C I
Z N C S U O R E F I C O V P D
A B E A D V E R S A R Y Z D F
F L Q P E C N E L U P O K L R
U C I D P G S G U P W P H G T
X X U A W Z Q W T N P D G F N

VOCIFEROUS
OPULENCE
SALIENT
ADVERSARY
WIZENED
BRIGAND
RAPPORT
ANARCHY
DISCORDANT
SERVILE

Word Search Game #7

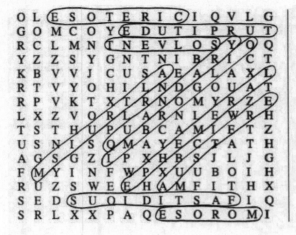

ESOTERIC
IMBROGLIO
QUANDARY
MOROSE
FASTIDIOUS
TURPITUDE
AUSTERE
SOLVENT
ALTRUISM
EPHEMERAL

Word Search Game #8

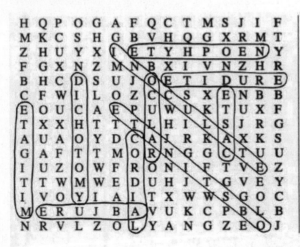

INOCULATE
MITIGATE
OCULAR
NEOPHYTE
ERUDITE
CORDIAL
ABJURE
CASTE
DICHOTOMY
OBSTINATE

Word Search Game #9

```
Y  J  C  L  S  C  O  T  A  Z  B  V  G  U  H
N  J  D  Y  T  I  R  A  P  S  I  D  L  G  O
A  B  G  C  W  G  Z  Y  C  G  S  I  I  D  R
L  U  X  U  Y  U  Q  Q  P  O  D  R  Z  E  G
Y  M  Y  J  J  O  B  G  S  Q  E  M  A  O  Z
S  G  E  Z  D  Y  F  L  X  T  Y  K  X  Q  T
D  I  P  I  X  P  Z  G  A  W  X  B  F  I  A
M  N  O  C  O  E  R  C  I  O  N  U  C  L  R
W  U  W  E  H  U  I  G  R  P  R  I  Q  H  C
S  N  W  U  R  R  C  S  V  T  I  B  V  T  H
D  D  H  U  T  K  Y  A  I  P  C  H  H  L  A
P  A  B  N  F  G  D  V  X  J  P  X  G  M  I
P  T  I  G  S  B  E  E  H  T  I  L  O  V  C
Y  E  K  K  D  N  E  J  W  M  O  H  J  Y  D
G  C  D  L  M  I  S  E  R  L  Y  J  L  D  B
```

ODIOUS
LITHE
INUNDATE
FURTIVE
EXPLICIT
MISERLY
INTRICATE
DISPARITY
ARCHAIC
COERCION

Word Search Game #10

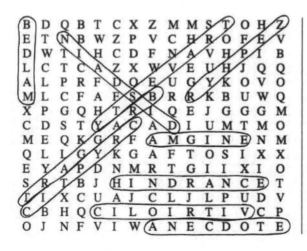

```
B  D  Q  B  T  C  X  Z  M  M  S  T  O  H  Z
E  T  N  B  W  Z  P  V  C  H  R  O  F  E  V
D  W  T  I  H  C  D  F  N  A  V  H  P  I  B
L  C  T  C  A  Z  X  W  E  U  H  J  Q  Q
A  L  P  R  F  D  O  E  U  G  Y  K  O  V  O
M  L  C  F  A  E  S  B  R  R  K  B  U  W  Q
X  P  G  Q  H  T  R  I  Q  E  J  G  G  G  M
C  D  S  T  Y  A  C  A  D  I  U  M  T  M  O
M  E  Q  K  G  R  F  A  M  G  I  N  E  N  M
Q  L  I  G  Y  K  G  A  F  T  O  S  I  X  X
E  Y  A  P  D  N  M  R  T  G  I  I  X  I  O
S  R  T  B  J  H  I  N  D  R  A  N  C  E  T
I  X  C  U  A  J  C  L  J  L  P  U  D  V
C  B  H  Q  C  I  L  O  I  R  T  I  V  C  P
O  J  N  F  V  I  W  A  N  E  C  D  O  T  E
```

VITRIOLIC
HINDRANCE
DISDAIN
BEDLAM
ZEPHYR
TRAVESTY
CRYPTIC
ANECDOTE
ENIGMA
BRAGGART

9 ▶ Matching Column Games

In this chapter, you'll learn to look carefully at similar-sounding (or similarly spelled) pairs of words to find the correct meaning for each.

Instructions

Draw a line to match the word in Column A with the definition in Column B. Be careful—these lists are made up of pairs of commonly confused words, and the games will be a little tricky.

Answers can be found at the end of the chapter.

Matching Column Game #1

A	B
allusion	practicing extreme self-denial; austerity
illusion	location, scene, or point of occurrence
aesthetic	expression of respect or affection; good wishes
ascetic	something that is misleading or deceptive
cite	occurring at the same time; running parallel
site	appreciation of beauty or art
compliment	indirect reference
complement	refer to or quote authoritatively; call upon officially
concurrent	following one after the other in order
consecutive	make something complete

Matching Column Game #2

A	B
connote	modest; having good moral judgment
denote	indifferent; not interested
discrete	someone who settles in a new country
discreet	associate; express indirectly or imply
disinterested	glue-like; gummy
uninterested	indicate; make known
emigrant	having an enormous appetite
immigrant	separate; individually distinct
glutinous	one who departs a country to settle elsewhere
gluttonous	impartial; unbiased

Matching Column Game #3

A	B
figuratively	symbolically; metaphorically
literally	(1) toward the front; (2) send on or pass along
foreword	writing materials; notepaper
forward	form; produce; create
stationary	unlawful
stationery	actually; word-for-word
comprise	to draw out (especially emotion or information)
compose	made up of; included within a particular scope
elicit	introductory note or preface
illicit	fixed; unmoving

Matching Column Game #4

A	B
inflammable	capable of being bought; corrupt through bribery
nonflammable	(1) one who founds or establishes; (2) give way; sink
founder	next-to-last
flounder	most remote; last; best or most extreme
penultimate	contrary or opposed; unfavorable
ultimate	having a feeling of intense dislike or repulsion
venial	unable to be set on fire
venal	minor; pardonable
adverse	able to be set on fire
averse	(1) a marine fish; (2) struggle or thrash about

Matching Column Game #5

A	B
empathy	give notice; tell
sympathy	tool used for making holes or removing loose material
appraise	feeling of loyalty or support for another
apprise	one who supervises conduct or morals; to suppress
augur	set a value or estimate the cost of something
auger	official reprimand or condemnation
censure	find similarities or resemblances
censor	find a degree of difference
compare	sharing another's emotions or feelings
contrast	a person who foretells events or sees the future

Matching Column Game #6

A	B
council	nonstop; continuing uninterrupted
counsel	an advisory or legislative body or group
continuous	recurring in rapid succession; occurring regularly
continual	(1) downward inclination; (2) deriving from ancestors
decent	advice, policy, or plan of action
descent	make less harmful or tense
defuse	frequency of occurrence
diffuse	happenings; events that lead to grave consequences
incidence	appropriate; free from immodesty or obscenity
incidents	not concentrated; spread out

Matching Column Game #7

A	B
insight	provide or obtain insurance; take precaution
incite	relating to an office or position
ensure	move to action; stir up
insure	suited for war; related to military life
marital	to make certain
martial	transparent; clear and precise
officious	of or relating to marriage
official	penetration; seeing the inner nature of something
perspicuous	kind; dutiful
perspicacious	acutely insightful and wise

Matching Column Game #8

A	B
proscribe	continue; follow a certain course
prescribe	height; quality or status gained by development
precede	recommend; specify with authority
proceed	twisting and turning; devious or indirect tactics
stature	excessively greedy or eager; having a large appetite
statute	unpleasant or painful
tortuous	condemn or forbid as harmful
torturous	law or legislative act
vociferous	be, go, or come ahead or in front of; surpass
voracious	blatant; conspicuous and offensive outcry

Matching Column Game #9

A	B
conscience	suggest; express or state indirectly
conscious	guess; deduce
eminent	awake; aware
imminent	able to be perceived or detected
imply	standing out or above in quality or position
infer	worthy of notice
notable	at hand; about to occur
noticeable	having no connection with an issue; unrelated
irreverent	moral sense of right and wrong
irrelevant	showing disrespect

Matching Column Game #10

A	B
convince	show off shamelessly
persuade	encourage; talk someone into something
flaunt	an educator in a position of high authority
flout	basic truth or belief; rule of personal conduct
principal	plead with; urge
principle	neither moral nor immoral
amoral	tease; taunt
immoral	to agree or be in accord
gibe	disregard; show scorn or contempt
jibe	unethical; morally objectionable

Answers

Matching Column Game #1

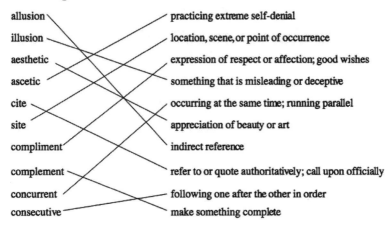

allusion	practicing extreme self-denial
illusion	location, scene, or point of occurrence
aesthetic	expression of respect or affection; good wishes
ascetic	something that is misleading or deceptive
cite	occurring at the same time; running parallel
site	appreciation of beauty or art
compliment	indirect reference
complement	refer to or quote authoritatively; call upon officially
concurrent	following one after the other in order
consecutive	make something complete

Matching Column Game #2

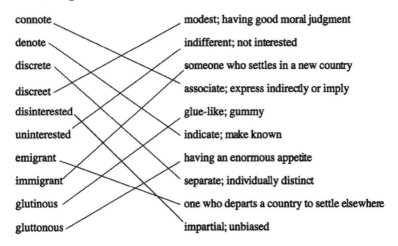

connote	modest; having good moral judgment
denote	indifferent; not interested
discrete	someone who settles in a new country
discreet	associate; express indirectly or imply
disinterested	glue-like; gummy
uninterested	indicate; make known
emigrant	having an enormous appetite
immigrant	separate; individually distinct
glutinous	one who departs a country to settle elsewhere
gluttonous	impartial; unbiased

Matching Column Game #3

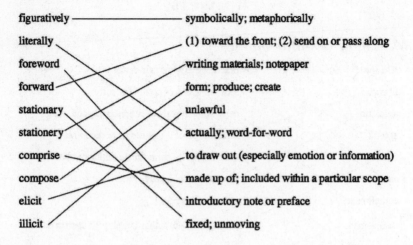

figuratively — symbolically; metaphorically

literally — (1) toward the front; (2) send on or pass along

foreword — writing materials; notepaper

forward — form; produce; create

stationary — unlawful

stationery — actually; word-for-word

comprise — to draw out (especially emotion or information)

compose — made up of; included within a particular scope

elicit — introductory note or preface

illicit — fixed; unmoving

Matching Column Game #4

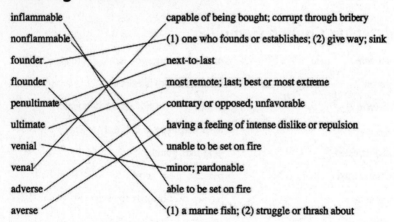

inflammable — capable of being bought; corrupt through bribery

nonflammable — (1) one who founds or establishes; (2) give way; sink

founder — next-to-last

flounder — most remote; last; best or most extreme

penultimate — contrary or opposed; unfavorable

ultimate — having a feeling of intense dislike or repulsion

venial — unable to be set on fire

venal — minor; pardonable

adverse — able to be set on fire

averse — (1) a marine fish; (2) struggle or thrash about

Matching Column Game #5

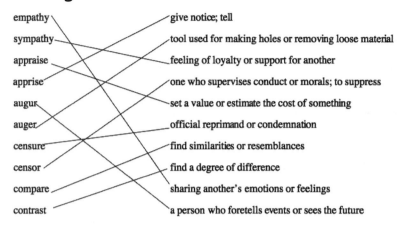

empathy	give notice; tell
sympathy	tool used for making holes or removing loose material
appraise	feeling of loyalty or support for another
apprise	one who supervises conduct or morals; to suppress
augur	set a value or estimate the cost of something
auger	official reprimand or condemnation
censure	find similarities or resemblances
censor	find a degree of difference
compare	sharing another's emotions or feelings
contrast	a person who foretells events or sees the future

Matching Column Game #6

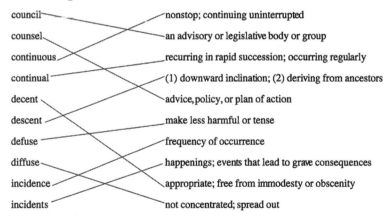

council	nonstop; continuing uninterrupted
counsel	an advisory or legislative body or group
continuous	recurring in rapid succession; occurring regularly
continual	(1) downward inclination; (2) deriving from ancestors
decent	advice, policy, or plan of action
descent	make less harmful or tense
defuse	frequency of occurrence
diffuse	happenings; events that lead to grave consequences
incidence	appropriate; free from immodesty or obscenity
incidents	not concentrated; spread out

Matching Column Game #7

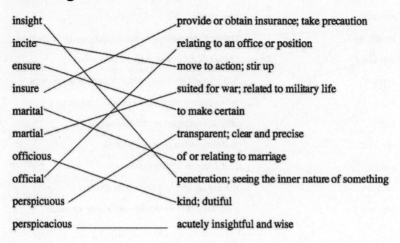

insight	provide or obtain insurance; take precaution
incite	relating to an office or position
ensure	move to action; stir up
insure	suited for war; related to military life
marital	to make certain
martial	transparent; clear and precise
officious	of or relating to marriage
official	penetration; seeing the inner nature of something
perspicuous	kind; dutiful
perspicacious _____	acutely insightful and wise

Matching Column Game #8

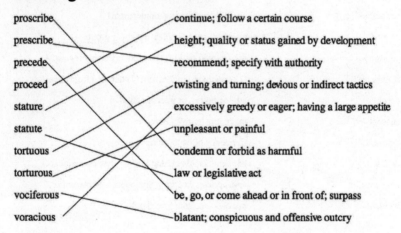

proscribe	continue; follow a certain course
prescribe	height; quality or status gained by development
precede	recommend; specify with authority
proceed	twisting and turning; devious or indirect tactics
stature	excessively greedy or eager; having a large appetite
statute	unpleasant or painful
tortuous	condemn or forbid as harmful
torturous	law or legislative act
vociferous	be, go, or come ahead or in front of; surpass
voracious	blatant; conspicuous and offensive outcry

Matching Column Game #9

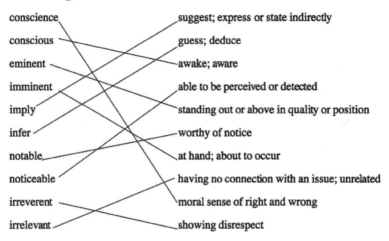

conscience	suggest; express or state indirectly
conscious	guess; deduce
eminent	awake; aware
imminent	able to be perceived or detected
imply	standing out or above in quality or position
infer	worthy of notice
notable	at hand; about to occur
noticeable	having no connection with an issue; unrelated
irreverent	moral sense of right and wrong
irrelevant	showing disrespect

Matching Column Game #10

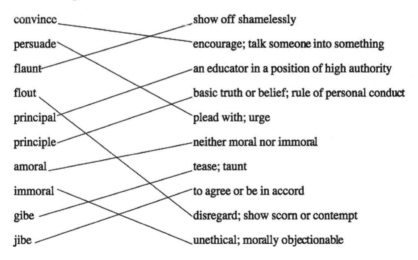

convince	show off shamelessly
persuade	encourage; talk someone into something
flaunt	an educator in a position of high authority
flout	basic truth or belief; rule of personal conduct
principal	plead with; urge
principle	neither moral nor immoral
amoral	tease; taunt
immoral	to agree or be in accord
gibe	disregard; show scorn or contempt
jibe	unethical; morally objectionable

10 ▶ Double-Word Puzzles

In this chapter, you will learn to remember definitions and spellings of ACT words. You'll identify a word by its meaning, and then spell it out without assistance.

Instructions

Use the definition provided to find each clue word. Write the word in the boxes next to each definition. Next, unscramble the letters in the circled boxes within the clue words to find a bonus vocabulary word.

If you get stuck, scan the word list on page 110 to see if you can figure out the word to match the definition. Be careful—some words in this chapter have similar definitions or spellings, and others have been used more than once.

Answers are found at the end of the chapter. Don't peek!

Hidden-Meaning Puzzle #1

1. deliberate; carefully thought out (10 letters)

2. sly or crafty (4 letters)

3. thin; not thick (6 letters)

4. exaggerated praise or flattery (9 letters)

5. sincerity and openness (6 letters)

6. loose robe (6 letters)

7. show or illustrate by example (9 letters)

8. act of going off-subject; turning attention away (10 letters)

9. conspicuously bad; scandalous (8 letters)

10. come between or step in (9 letters)

Bonus: words that mean the opposite of what one thinks or assumes

Hidden-Meaning Puzzle #2

1. goad or provoke (9 letters)

2. exercising discretion and sound judgment (7 letters)

3. sly or crafty (4 letters)

4. remedy; something that counteracts (8 letters)

5. complicated (9 letters)

6. get or gather together (7 letters)

7. someone who excels at making speeches (6 letters)

8. make movements or gestures while speaking (11 letters)

9. make official (6 letters)

10. using few words; brief (8 letters)

Bonus: careful; watchful

Hidden-Meaning Puzzle #3

1. never giving up (11 letters)

2. feel or show deep respect (8 letters)

3. complicated; long-winded (10 letters)

4. quiet; not inclined to speak (8 letters)

5. to give in to or fall under the influence of something (7 letters)

6. careful and organized (10 letters)

7. satisfy; please (7 letters)

8. express a negative opinion (9 letters)

9. kind (10 letters)

10. maintain or assert (7 letters)

Bonus: changing repeatedly

Hidden-Meaning Puzzle #4

1. belittle; disparage (9 letters)

2. praise; commend (5 letters)

3. supply or sell (6 letters)

4. moving apart in different directions; deviating (9 letters)

5. calmness in mind or bearing (9 letters)

6. outside edge of an area (9 letters)

7. reverse in position or order (6 letters)

8. transformation (11 letters)

9. easily tricked or deceived (8 letters)

10. deceitful; based on false or misleading information (10 letters)

Bonus: truth or accuracy

Hidden-Meaning Puzzle #5

1. breaking up or scattering; spreading widely (10 letters)

2. cease to consider (7 letters)

3. act of being or feeling suspicious or fearful (12 letters)

4. prediction, omen, or sense of doom (10 letters)

5. treat something as acceptable or understandable (7 letters)

6. reasonable and logical (9 letters)

7. extremely wicked (9 letters)

8. briefly passing through (9 letters)

9. shortness; conciseness (7 letters)

10. glowing (11 letters)

Bonus: craftsperson

Hidden-Meaning Puzzle #6

1. relationship or affinity between people (7 letters)

2. closeness (9 letters)

3. uncertain; capable of different meanings (9 letters)

4. possible; doable (8 letters)

5. burden or responsibility (4 letters)

6. assuming too much (12 letters)

7. quality or state of being new (7 letters)

8. refuse to accept (9 letters)

9. manipulate; use to one's own advantage (7 letters)

10. disdainful; stuck up (7 letters)

Bonus: someone who questions or doubts

Hidden-Meaning Puzzle #7

1. arrangement by rank or position (9 letters)

2. not hurtful; harmless (9 letters)

3. laud; praise; glorify (5 letters)

4. act of not caring; being indifferent (11 letters)

5. rudeness (9 letters)

6. not essential (10 letters)

7. hindrance (9 letters)

8. state of dishonor or shame (11 letters)

9. cause to continue (10 letters)

10. fair and equal; having good judgment or common sense (9 letters)

Bonus: someone who goes against accepted authority

Hidden-Meaning Puzzle #8

1. remarkable development or event (10 letters)

2. faint trace or spark (9 letters)

3. glowing brightly; radiant (8 letters)

4. urge or force to action (5 letters)

5. event that occurs at a critical time (8 letters)

6. exaggerated opinion of one's own importance (7 letters)

7. willingness or readiness to believe (9 letters)

8. accurate; exact (10 letters)

9. state of being isolated or detached (10 letters)

10. praise, glorify, or honor (4 letters)

Bonus: using humor to show political or societal faults

Hidden-Meaning Puzzle #9

1. ambiguous, indirect, and wordy language (14 letters)

2. set a value or estimate the cost of something (8 letters)

3. specify; define (9 letters)

4. cultural, intellectual or moral tendencies of an era (9 letters)

5. showy; conspicuous (12 letters)

6. accidental; unintentional (11 letters)

7. disintegration or destruction caused by chemical action (9 letters)

8. limited; unsophisticated (10 letters)

9. press or squeeze thoroughly (5 letters)

10. cause to calm (7 letters)

Bonus: using few words in writing or speech

Hidden-Meaning Puzzle #10

1. showing much respect (8 letters)

2. put in danger; threaten (10 letters)

3. feeling or showing acceptance of something unpleasant (8 letters)

4. strict (9 letters)

5. arrogant or haughty (12 letters)

6. strength or determination (5 letters)

7. often but not readily or steadily (8 letters)

8. line of people waiting in order of arrival (5 letters)

9. unnecessary (9 letters)

10. existing in every part of something (9 letters)

Bonus: examine closely

Word List for Chapter 10

adulation	contend	equivocal	haughty
antidote	convoluted	exalt	hierarchy
appraise	corrosion	exemplify	iconoclast
apprehension	credulity	exploit	ignominious
artisan	delineate	extol	impel
benevolent	deprecate	extraneous	impudence
brevity	deterrent	fallacious	inadvertent
calculated	digression	feasible	innocuous
candor	dismiss	flagrant	instigate
circumlocution	disparage	foreboding	insularity
compile	dispersion	gesticulate	intervene
composure	divergent	gratify	intricate
condone	egotism	gullible	invert

ironic	onus	queue	succumb
jeopardize	orator	ratify	supercilious
judicious	ostentatious	redundant	taciturn
juncture	periphery	repudiate	transient
kimono	permutation	resigned	unrelenting
kinship	perpetuate	resplendent	vacillate
knead	pervasive	reverent	venerate
laconic	phenomenon	satirical	veracity
laud	placate	scintilla	vigor
luminous	pragmatic	scrutinize	wary
methodical	presumptuous	skeptic	wily
meticulous	provincial	sparse	zeitgeist
nefarious	proximity	sporadic	
nonchalance	prudent	stringent	
novelty	purvey	succinct	

Answers

Hidden-Meaning Puzzle #1

1. calculated
2. wily
3. sparse
4. adulation
5. candor
6. kimono
7. exemplify
8. digression
9. flagrant
10. intervene

Bonus: ironic

Hidden-Meaning Puzzle #2

1. instigate
2. prudent
3. wily
4. antidote
5. intricate
6. compile
7. orator
8. gesticulate
9. ratify
10. succinct

Bonus: wary

Hidden-Meaning Puzzle #3

1. unrelenting
2. venerate
3. convoluted
4. taciturn
5. succumb
6. methodical
7. gratify
8. disparage
9. benevolent
10. contend

Bonus: vacillate

Hidden-Meaning Puzzle #4

1. deprecate
2. extol
3. purvey
4. divergent
5. composure
6. periphery
7. invert
8. permutation
9. gullible
10. fallacious

Bonus: veracity

Hidden-Meaning Puzzle #5

1. dispersion
2. dismiss
3. apprehension
4. foreboding
5. condone
6. pragmatic
7. nefarious
8. transient
9. brevity
10. resplendent

Bonus: artisan

Hidden-Meaning Puzzle #6

1. kinship
2. proximity
3. equivocal
4. feasible
5. onus
6. presumptuous
7. novelty
8. repudiate
9. exploit
10. haughty

Bonus: skeptic

Hidden-Meaning Puzzle #7

1. hierarchy
2. innocuous
3. exalt
4. nonchalance
5. impudence
6. extraneous
7. deterrent
8. ignominious
9. perpetuate
10. judicious

Bonus: iconoclast

Hidden-Meaning Puzzle #8

1. phenomenon
2. scintilla
3. luminous
4. impel
5. juncture
6. egotism
7. credulity
8. meticulous
9. insularity
10. laud

Bonus: satirical

Hidden-Meaning Puzzle #9

1. circumlocution
2. appraise
3. delineate
4. zeitgeist
5. ostentatious
6. inadvertent
7. corrosion
8. provincial
9. knead
10. placate

Bonus: laconic

Hidden-Meaning Puzzle #10

1. reverent
2. jeopardize
3. resigned
4. stringent
5. supercilious
6. vigor
7. sporadic
8. queue
9. redundant
10. pervasive

Bonus: scrutinize

11

▶ **Cryptograms**

In this chapter, you will learn the spellings and definitions of common ACT vocabulary words.

Instructions

Fill in numbers 1 through 26, in order, in the hint box for each game. You will then have a number corresponding to each letter for the entire alphabet.

Then, use these letter-number pairs to solve each definition. Once you've figured out the definition, unscramble each word.

Answers are found at the back of the chapter. Don't peek!

Cryptogram #1

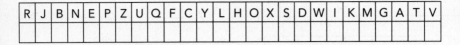

R	J	B	N	E	P	Z	U	Q	F	C	Y	L	H	O	X	S	D	W	I	K	M	G	A	T	V

___ ___ ___ ___ ___   ___ ___ ___ ___
13 24 1 23 5   10 20 1   5

Unscramble: F O R C T I O N L A G A N

Cryptogram #2

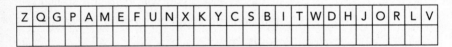

Z	Q	G	P	A	M	E	F	U	N	X	K	Y	C	S	B	I	T	W	D	H	J	O	R	L	V

___ ___ ___ ___ ___ ___ ___ ___ ___   ___ ___ ___ ___ ___ ___
 8   5 10   5 18 17 14   5 25   4   7 24 15 23 10

Unscramble: T O L A Z E

Cryptogram #3

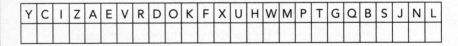

Y	C	I	Z	A	E	V	R	D	O	K	F	X	U	H	W	M	P	T	G	Q	B	S	J	N	L

___ ___ ___ ___ ___   ___ ___   ___ ___ ___ ___ ___
23   6   3   4   6   22   1   12 10   8   2   6

Unscramble: P U R S U

Cryptogram #4

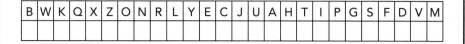

B	W	K	Q	X	Z	O	N	R	L	Y	E	C	J	U	A	H	T	I	P	G	S	F	D	V	M

$$\overline{22} \;\; \overline{7} \;\; \overline{26} \;\; \overline{12} \;\; \overline{7} \;\; \overline{8} \;\; \overline{12} \qquad \overline{2} \;\; \overline{17} \;\; \overline{7}$$

$$\overline{7} \;\; \overline{20} \;\; \overline{20} \;\; \overline{7} \;\; \overline{22} \;\; \overline{12} \;\; \overline{22} \qquad \overline{2} \;\; \overline{16} \;\; \overline{9}$$

Unscramble: F I S T I P A C

Cryptogram #5

B	F	J	O	N	Q	Z	T	I	R	P	C	D	L	K	G	S	V	A	H	U	M	W	Y	E	X

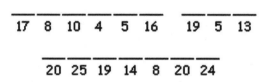

$$\overline{17} \;\; \overline{8} \;\; \overline{10} \;\; \overline{4} \;\; \overline{5} \;\; \overline{16} \qquad \overline{19} \;\; \overline{5} \;\; \overline{13}$$

$$\overline{20} \;\; \overline{25} \;\; \overline{19} \;\; \overline{14} \;\; \overline{8} \;\; \overline{20} \;\; \overline{24}$$

Unscramble: T R O U B S

Cryptogram #6

C	Z	O	B	W	P	G	D	E	Y	Q	F	L	X	U	V	N	S	M	K	H	A	T	I	J	R

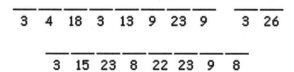

$$\overline{3} \;\; \overline{4} \;\; \overline{18} \;\; \overline{3} \;\; \overline{13} \;\; \overline{9} \;\; \overline{23} \;\; \overline{9} \qquad \overline{3} \;\; \overline{26}$$

$$\overline{3} \;\; \overline{15} \;\; \overline{23} \;\; \overline{8} \;\; \overline{22} \;\; \overline{23} \;\; \overline{9} \;\; \overline{8}$$

Unscramble: Q U A D T I E N T A

Cryptogram #7

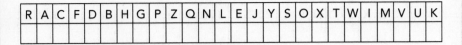

R	A	C	F	D	B	H	G	P	Z	Q	N	L	E	J	Y	S	O	X	T	W	I	M	V	U	K

22 23 9 13 18 1 14   18 1   6 14 8

Unscramble: C H E E S E B

Cryptogram #8

D	G	I	L	H	C	K	B	J	M	E	S	P	Q	A	Z	X	O	R	U	Y	W	F	N	T	V

8 15 23 23 4 11   18 19

6 18 24 23 20 12 11

Unscramble: C O U F N D O N

Cryptogram #9

A	T	C	D	Y	H	E	B	G	J	N	M	K	O	Z	X	U	V	P	W	R	L	S	I	Q	F

23 5 23 2 7 12   14 26

8 7 22 24 7 26 23

Unscramble: C R I T E N D O

Cryptogram #10

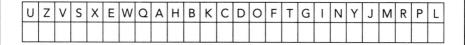

U	Z	V	S	X	E	W	Q	A	H	B	K	C	D	O	F	T	G	I	N	Y	J	M	R	P	L

20 15 17   4 6 24 19 15 1 4   :

4 19 26 26 21

Unscramble: O F U S L O V R I

Answers

Cryptogram #1
large fire
CONFLAGRATION

Cryptogram #2
fanatical person
ZEALOT

Cryptogram #3
seize by force
USURP

Cryptogram #4
someone who opposes war
PACIFIST

Cryptogram #5
strong and healthy
ROBUST

Cryptogram #6
obsolete or outdated
ANTIQUATED

Cryptogram #7
implore or beg
BESEECH

Cryptogram #8
baffle or confuse
CONFOUND

Cryptogram #9
system of beliefs
DOCTRINE

Cryptogram #10
not serious: silly
FRIVOLOUS

III

SET A FOOLPROOF STRATEGY

12 ▶ Planning and Preparing

Congratulations! You've finished the games in this book—which means you've taken a big step in improving your vocabulary skills. However, you may still have some time before the big day, right? Let's look at some more preparation you can do, to make sure your score is the absolute best it can be.

Six Months Before Test Day

So, you've got some time before the ACT exam. That's great! Read on for some additional things you can do to prepare yourself for the big day—from supersizing your vocabulary to learning the ins and outs of the exam and making sure you're in good shape—both physically and mentally—on the day of the test.

Keep Up the Vocab Workout

By now you're aware that a good working vocabulary is an important asset on the English sections of the ACT. But did you know that the best way to learn vocabulary is also the easiest? Simply keep an eye out for unfamiliar words, add them to a running list, and then set aside a few minutes each day to learn some of the words on that list.

DECONSTRUCT, DECONSTRUCT, DECONSTRUCT

When learning new words, remember to break them down into roots, prefixes, and suffixes (as you learned in Chapters 1 through 3). You'll be surprised to see how quickly knowing these will help you figure out definitions—and increase your vocabulary!

Let's figure it out. How much time do you have until you take the exam? Is it a month, three months, a year? Whatever the length of time, you still have a chance to substantially improve your vocabulary before sitting down with that test booklet.

So here's what you do. Count out the number of days before test day. (Don't count the night before—you'll be busy resting and rewarding yourself that night. See "The Night Before Test Day" in this chapter for more details.) Then, multiply the number of days by five. The result is the number of new vocabulary words you'll know before the exam—by learning just five words a day. You can handle that, right? Of course you can!

VOCAB IN A FLASH

One easy way to learn your five new words per day is to use flashcards. Write a word on one side and the definition on the other, and keep the cards with you to practice whenever you have spare time. You can use them to study alone, or quiz a friend—then have that friend quiz you. Flashcards are a great way to get in some study time anywhere. (If you're a techie or the kind of person who carries a mobile device at all times, check out some of the free flashcard apps available.)

Remember to be on the lookout for new words everywhere. Jot down unfamiliar words you see on signs, hear in conversations, or come across while reading your favorite magazines. Make sure your new words list is always with you, so you can keep track of the ones you've learned and the ones you have on deck for the next time you have some time to kill!

Familiarize Yourself with the Exam

One big advantage you can give yourself on the day of the test is to know exactly what to expect, from how the exam is structured to approximately how long it will take you to complete each section, when to spend time figuring out an answer, and when to just make an educated guess. Fortunately, there are lots of practice tools out there that can help you do just that.

TALK IT OUT

When you learn a new word, try to use it as soon as you can. Practical knowledge—using something you've learned in the real world—is often the best way to really integrate something into your mind. So talk to your friends, your family, and your teachers using ACT words—to help you remember those words when it counts. Work these words into e-mails and essays. See how many people can keep up with your vocab skills!

Books

You can find the most up-to-date practice books in your local library or in most bookstores. If you decide to use books to take practice exams, it's especially important to make sure that you're giving yourself the same amount of time to complete each section as you'll get on the day of the test. You can find some suggestions for good books in the Resources section on page 149.

Online

Another great way to practice for the ACT exam is to take an actual practice exam online. These exams often consist of actual questions used on past exams. There are lots of practice tests available on the

Internet—some are free, and others can be accessed for a fee. Some other suggestions for good practice sites are located in the Resources section on page 149.

Time Management

While you're taking practice tests, be sure to keep an eye on the time. The basic rule of ACT test taking is to allow yourself one minute per question; however, depending on your strengths, some questions will take you less time, and others will take more. Don't consider the "one-minute rule" to be hard and fast, but do be aware of the amount of time you're taking—and don't spend too much time on any one question.

When working on a question you're not sure of, be sure to eliminate wrong answer choices wherever you can. Cross out the ones you know are wrong on the test sheet so you can concentrate on the remaining possibilities, giving yourself a better chance at finding the right answer.

And don't forget that you can always go back and revisit questions if you come to the end of a section before time is up. Just circle the number of the question so you can find it easily if you have extra time at the end to go back to it.

Play to Your Strengths

You know better than anyone else what comes easily for you, and what you have to work hard on. So, if one type of question in a particular section is easier for you than another, skip right to it and answer those questions first. Answer the easy questions first and save the ones you find harder for last!

A Few Weeks Before Test Day

As test day looms closer, you may start to feel a bit of panic set in. Don't worry, that's normal. Besides, you have nothing to worry about because you've been preparing all along. So take a deep breath and relax!

Schedule Study Time

One way to really set your mind at ease is to put together a study schedule for the next few weeks leading up to the exam. Try to map out a half hour to an hour a day, and decide what you'll be working on in advance. Then, when you've completed your study session, stop! Studying regularly in small intervals is often more effective than trying to cram too much information into long, sleepless nights. When your allotted study time is up, close your book, turn off the computer, and go do something fun.

Step Away from the Chips!

You've probably heard that the best way to prepare yourself for anything stressful is to be sure that you're in good health. Lots of us tend to reach for the snacks while studying—and even more so when feeling stressed out over a big exam—but it goes without saying that healthy foods are best for keeping your mind and body in tip-top shape.

And speaking of shape, you know what else is a great stress-buster? Exercise. See Chapter 13 for more details, but the fact is that regular exercise helps keep the mind alert, reduces fatigue, and results in a better night's sleep.

A Few Days Before Test Day

A few days before the exam is the best time for some last-minute brush-ups. Grab your book or log on to your computer and take a practice exam one final time. Focus on your problem areas, and give yourself a little extra study time in those areas. Review everything you know about the ACT exam to make sure that there will be absolutely no surprises on test day.

Do a Dry Run

It's not only a good idea to be as familiar as you can be with the test itself, but it's also smart to know exactly where you'll be going—and how you'll be getting there—on the day of the test, so you don't wake up in a panic about it. Find out where your test center is located, and go there at the same time and day of the week as your exam is scheduled. Take the same mode of transportation you will be using on exam day, so you can get a good sense ahead of time, learn about unexplained glitches in Google Maps, notice any construction that may force you to take a detour, or discover unforeseen public transportation issues.

Review Test-Taking Policies
There are very specific guidelines that determine what you can and can't bring into the test center, as well as security and fairness regulations in place at the test centers. Familiarize yourself with them, so you know what you can expect when you arrive.

Get Organized
Gather together everything you will need the day of the test and put it in a safe place (see Chapter 14 for a checklist of essential items). That way, you won't have to worry about rushing around before you leave in the morning, looking for your admission ticket or a calculator.

The Day Before Test Day

You've worked hard, and your efforts are about to pay off. But it's the day before the exam, and you're going to work really hard tomorrow to do the best you can on the ACT. You're as ready as you'll ever be, so take this opportunity to give yourself a well-deserved break.

Tonight, your assignment is to watch a good movie, spend some time with your friends, play a video game or board game with family members, or do another fun and relaxing activity. Be sure to get to bed early enough to guarantee a full night's rest. The only thing you should not do is think about the ACT exam.

On the Big Day

It's finally here! The day you've been preparing for all these weeks and months has arrived, but don't worry. You've studied, you've learned how the test is administered and what to look for, and you know exactly how long it's going to take to get to the test center. So you have nothing at all to worry about. Just concentrate on doing your best on the exam.

Prepare with Protein

You've got a long day ahead of you, so be sure to start the morning right. Eat a good breakfast, which ideally should be rich in protein. (It's widely believed that protein helps increase alertness and response time.) Some good choices are eggs, grains, nuts, or dairy products such as yogurt or cottage cheese. Whatever you choose, make sure to eat enough. You don't want everyone to hear your stomach growling half an hour into the exam.

Load Up on Layers

You won't have any control over the temperature in the room in which you'll be sitting for the next several hours, and the last thing you need is to be distracted by chattering teeth or sweat pooling across your forehead. Wear something comfortable, but be sure to include layers, so you're guaranteed not to be too hot or too warm while you're taking the test.

Keep an Eye on the Clock

Make sure that you give yourself plenty of time to get to the test center, even if major traffic or a natural disaster suddenly decides to get in your way. You don't want to be rushing into the room at the last minute.

That's it! You're ready to go out there and get a great score on the ACT. Just one final thing—make sure you have a post-test celebration in mind, because you definitely deserve it.

Good luck!

13 ▶ Anxiety-Busting Exercises

Let's face it. As well prepared as you are for your test, you might be feeling some stress and anxiety about it. This is normal—anxiety is a common response to difficult situations, and it happens to many people.

There are many things you can do to combat stress and anxiety, and ensure that you arrive at the test center relaxed and ready to take on the exam. The first thing to do is remind yourself that you've studied and practiced, so you're undeniably ready for the challenge. Feel confident in the knowledge that, unlike many others, you're walking into that exam room prepared for what lies ahead.

But sometimes knowing that you're ready isn't enough. In that case, there are some simple exercises you can do to keep yourself calm and collected. These exercises can help you deal with stress, and can be done anywhere, anytime. Whenever you feel yourself starting to panic about the upcoming exam, just take some time to do one of the following.

Deep Breathing

Just breathe in and out? Really? Yes, it's that simple. Take a few minutes to sit back, close your eyes, and concentrate on taking deep, regular breaths. This simple act will help slow your heart rate and make you feel calmer.

Muscle Relaxation

Sit in a chair or on the floor, or lie on your bed. Begin by tensing each of your muscles for a count of ten, then slowly relaxing them. Work from your toes up to your shoulders, and then back down again. You'll feel more rested and relaxed in no time.

Visualization

It may sound silly, but many people believe that they do better in stressful situations and accomplish goals more easily if they've first pictured themselves succeeding. So, take a few minutes to sit back, relax, and imagine yourself walking into the test center. You've prepared, you've got all your materials with you, you've slept well and eaten a good breakfast, and you're armed with the knowledge you need to ace the test. Now, picture yourself leaning over the test booklet, flipping confidently through it, knowing some answers right away, making educated guesses about others, and knowing that it's okay to leave some blank if you really have no idea. Then picture yourself confidently closing the booklet, standing up, and heading out to celebrate when you're done. It doesn't seem so bad now, does it?

Meditation

The idea behind meditation is to relax your body while concentrating on one thing. Sit or lie in a comfortable position, close your eyes, and try thinking about a positive outcome on the exam. Breathe deeply in and out for ten minutes. You'll find that you feel more relaxed and refreshed afterward.

If you're familiar with the moves, yoga is also a great way to relax your body and prepare your mind to concentrate. But don't strain your muscles doing anything you're not used to—the point here is to relax, not to put undue stress on your body.

Exercise

Exercise is another great way to get rid of stress. But exercise doesn't have to consist of lifting weights or running on the treadmill at the gym; it can be a game of touch football with your friends, playing with your dog in the park, or even some time spent dancing to your favorite songs in your room. Work up a sweat and put those anxious thoughts out of your mind. Your body—and your brain—will thank you for it!

Walk Away from Naysayers

Sometimes it helps to vent about a stressful situation to family or friends, but other times it can add to your anxiety. If someone you know is constantly complaining about how hard the ACT exam is, or how she knows she's going to crash and burn, it's okay to change the subject. Really. Just shrug and say that all you can do is prepare, and then go do exactly that.

Regardless of what method you choose, the important thing to remember is to not let anxiety put you on edge before the exam. Keep in mind that the hardest part of taking the ACT is often the time leading up to the exam itself. Just do the best you can, and don't worry about anything else.

14 ▶ Test-Day Checklist

What to Bring

☐ photo ID
☐ test center admission ticket
☐ sharpened Number 2 pencils
☐ eraser
☐ calculator (graphing, scientific, or four-function ONLY) with
  extra batteries
☐ watch (with no audio alerts)

What NOT to Bring

☐ tobacco in any form
☐ mobile phone
☐ iPod, MP3 player, or audio device
☐ iPad, netbook, or laptop computer
☐ BlackBerry, mobile organizer, or PDA
☐ highlighters, markers, pens, or colored pencils
☐ notes or other paper

☐ books
☐ camera or photographic equipment

What to Do

☐ eat a good breakfast
☐ dress in layers so you're comfortable in the exam room
☐ pack some water and a healthy snack for your break
☐ leave home early, so you are sure to arrive on time, even if there's traffic

Glossary

A

abjure formally reject or renounce

abdicate give up a position of leadership

abominable detestable

abridge shorten or edit down while keeping the essential elements

abstemious voluntary restraint (especially from consuming food and drink)

abstruse incomprehensible; difficult to penetrate

acerbic sour or bitter

adulation exaggerated praise or flattery

adversary opponent

adversity unfavorable or oppositional conditions or events

advocate (1) argue in favor of something; (2) person who argues in favor of something

aesthetic appreciation of beauty or art

affable warm and friendly

affirmation declaration or assertion of truth

alleviate relieve; make less severe

allusion indirect reference

aloof remote or removed; standoffish

altruism unselfish concern for others; self-sacrifice

amalgam mixture of different elements

ambivalent undecided; unclear

ameliorate make better

amicable agreeable; friendly

anachronism something that belongs to another time

analogous similar or equivalent; showing likeness

anarchy state of lawlessness and disorder in the absence of a government

anecdote short story or account of something interesting

animosity resentment or hostility; feeling of ill will

anomalous odd; not fitting a particular pattern

antagonism active opposition or dislike

antidote remedy; something that counteracts

antiquated obsolete or outdated

apathy lack of energy or interest

appease pacify; make quiet or calm

appraise set a value or estimate the cost of something

apprehension act of being or feeling suspicious or fearful

apprenticeship time spent as a beginner learning a trade or career from an expert

apprise give notice; tell

archaic old-fashioned; outdated

arrogance unwarranted pride; superiority

articulate express well in words

artifact something created by humans and remaining from a particular era

artisan craftsperson

augment increase or enlarge

augur person who foretells events or sees the future

B

bedlam madhouse; scene of uproar and confusion

belie misrepresent or give a false impression

beneficial helpful

benevolent kind

benign mild or gentle

beseech implore or beg

bibulous tendency to consume beverages in large quantities

blasé sophisticated; unconcerned with pleasure or excitement

blatant obvious

blithe joyous

bombastic too elaborate; exaggerated

braggart someone who boasts or brags

brevity shortness; conciseness

brigand someone who lives by plundering or theft

brusque blunt or rude in manner or speech

bucolic of or related to the countryside and farming

bumptious aggressively conceited and presumptuous

buoyant lighthearted; high-spirited

bureaucracy obstruction by insistence on unnecessary procedures or regulations

C

cajole wheedle; coax; persuade

calculated deliberate; carefully thought out

callous cruel; unfeeling

candor sincerity and openness

cantankerous ill-tempered; cranky

capricious fickle; changing on a whim

caste hereditary social class

censorious harshly critical

censure official reprimand or condemnation

cerebral involving intellect, rather than emotion

chicanery trickery

chide scold

churlish ill-mannered; rude

circumlocution ambiguous, indirect, and wordy language

circumspect careful to consider all feelings and consequences; prudent

cite refer to or quote authoritatively; call upon officially

coercion using force to cause something to occur; compelling through authority

cohesive forming a whole; sticking together

compile get or gather together

complacency self-satisfaction; contentment

complement make something complete

compliance conformity

compliment expression of respect or affection; good wishes

compose form; produce; create

composure calmness in mind or bearing

comprehensive all-inclusive

concede admit; surrender or relinquish

conciliatory compromising; appeasing

concise brief; to-the-point

concur act together; agree

condone treat something as acceptable or understandable

concurrent occurring at the same time; running parallel

condone treat something as acceptable or understandable

conflagration large fire

confound baffle or confuse

congenial compatible; friendly

consensus agreement among the members of a group

consolidation unification or combination into a whole

constituency body of voters with shared interests, identity, or goals

constraint limit or restriction

contend maintain or assert

contentious inclined to dispute or disagree

conviction (1) unshakeable belief (2) final judgment of guilty in a criminal case

convivial friendly; sociable

convoluted complicated; long-winded

cordial politely warm and friendly

corroborate confirm; validate

corrosion disintegration or destruction caused by chemical action

cosmopolitan sophisticated; worldly

credulity willingness or readiness to believe

criterion standard or basis for comparison

cryptic hidden; mysterious

cursory without attention for detail; not thorough

curtail restrict; cut short

D

debacle sudden, disastrous collapse or downfall

decorum behavior that is proper or correct

deference courteous respect or regard for the feelings of others

degradation act of reducing or breaking down

delineate specify; define

denounce speak out against someone or something

depravity moral corruption

deprecate belittle; disparage

deride ridicule; show contempt for

despondent without hope

deterrent hindrance

detrimental damaging

devious not straightforward; dishonest or sneaky

devise invent; create

dichotomy division into two contradictory groups

didactic excessively instructional

diffuse not concentrated; spread out

digression act of going off-subject; turning attention away

diligence conscientiousness; perseverance

diminution decline; decrease

discerning having good judgment; showing insight and understanding

discordant quarrelsome; disagreeing

discrepancy inconsistency; conflicting facts or claims

discriminating able to perceive small differences in similar things

disdain contempt

dismiss cease to consider

disparage express a negative opinion

disparity inequality or difference

dispersion breaking up or scattering; spreading widely

disputatious showing an inclination to disagree

disseminate circulate; cause to become widely known

divergent moving apart in different directions; deviating

doctrine system of beliefs

dogmatic strongly expressing beliefs as if they were facts

dubious doubtful

duplicity deception

E

eclectic mixed style; composed of elements drawn from different sources

effervescent lively; bubbly

effusive burbling; enthusiastic

egotism exaggerated opinion of one's own importance

egress place of exit

elated thrilled; overjoyed

elite privileged

elocution correct and proper inflection and intonation in speech

eloquence characterized by powerful and effective speech

elusive skillful at avoiding capture or comprehension

embellish make beautiful or elegant with ornamentation

eminent above others in quality or position

emulate imitate or copy

endorse (1) sign; (2) support

enhance increase or heighten

enigma puzzle; riddle

enmity hostility

enterprising displaying initiative, daring, and readiness to take on new projects

ephemeral short-lived

epistolary of or relating to letters and letter-writing

epitome a typical example

equivocal uncertain; capable of different meanings

erroneous wrong

erudite showing vast knowledge; learned

esoteric limited to a small circle; requiring specialized information

euphemism substitution of an inoffensive term to replace a harsher or more distasteful one

exacerbate make worse

exalt laud; praise; glorify

exemplary worthy of imitation

exemplify show or illustrate by example

exhaustive including every possible element; comprehensive; complete

exhilarating thrilling; lively or cheerful

exonerate acquit; free from accusation or blame

expedient easy or simple method; appropriate for a particular circumstance

expedite speed up a process

explicit very clear and direct

exploit manipulate; use to one's own advantage

extol praise; commend

extraneous not essential

extricate release from entanglement or difficulty

exuberance joyful enthusiasm

F

facilitate make easier; help

facsimile exact copy or reproduction

fallacious deceitful; based on false or misleading information

famish suffer from extreme hunger; starve

fanaticism excessive intolerance of opposing views

fastidious paying careful attention to detail

feasible possible; doable

fervor ardor; excitement

flagrant conspicuously bad; scandalous

florid excessively elaborate or showy; flowery

flout disregard; show scorn or contempt

foraging searching for provisions; collecting food

foreboding prediction, omen, or sense of doom

forfeit surrender; lose

franchise authorization to sell a particular product or service

frivolous not serious; silly

frugality the act of being economical or thrifty

furtive secret; quietly cautious

fusion mixture; melding

G

gamut entire series or range

garrulous talkative

genteel having an elegant or superior quality

germane relevant and appropriate

gesticulate make movements or gestures while speaking

glutinous glue-like; gummy

gluttonous having an enormous appetite

grandiose overly large and impressive

gratify satisfy; please

gratuitous unnecessary or unwarranted

gregarious sociable; friendly

guile shrewdness; craftiness

gullible easily tricked or deceived

H

halcyon idyllically calm and peaceful

haughty disdainful; stuck up

hedonist concerned with or motivated by pleasure

heinous extremely wicked; reprehensible

heresy opinions that are controversial or unorthodox

hermetic completely sealed; airtight

hierarchy arrangement by rank or position

hindrance something that interferes with or delays action or progress

homogenous all alike or similar

honorarium compensation for a professional service

hypocritical deceptive; pretending to be good or virtuous

hypothetical based on guesswork; not proven

I

iconoclast someone who goes against accepted authority

idiosyncrasy quirk or unique trait

ignominious state of dishonor or shame

imbibe absorb; drink

imbroglio complicated situation; entanglement

immutable unable to be changed or varied

impeccable faultless; perfect

impecunious habitually lacking money; poor

impede get in the way; hinder

impel urge or force to action

impermeable not easily penetrated; not permitting passage (especially of a liquid)

implausible unlikely; dubious

impudence rudeness

inadvertent accidental; unintentional

inane pointless; silly

incisive acute; keen

incite motivate; provoke or stir up

incongruous lacking in harmony or compatibility

incorrigible unable to be corrected through punishment

incumbent (1) current holder of a particular office; (2) necessary or moral obligation

indict formally accuse of a crime

induce cause to do or act

industrious hard-working; diligent

inept clumsy or inexpert

inert unable to move

ingenious resourceful, clever

innocuous not hurtful; harmless

inoculate introduce a microorganism in order to treat or prevent a disease; vaccinate

insipid bland or flavorless; boring

insouciant carefree; sociable

instigate goad or provoke

insularity state of being isolated or detached

insurgent rebellious

integrity moral soundness

intervene come between or step in

intrepid fearless

intricate complicated

inundate overwhelm

invert reverse in position or order

ironic words that mean the opposite of what one thinks or assumes

irrefutable cannot be proved wrong

J

jeopardize put into danger; threaten

jocund cheerful

jovial jolly; full of good humor

jubilant extremely joyful

judicious fair and equal; having good judgment or common sense

junction place where two or more things come together; being joined

juncture event that occurs at a critical time

jurisprudence philosophy, science, and study of law

justification acceptable reason or excuse for doing something

K

kimono loose robe

kinship relationship or affinity between people

knavery being tricky or dishonest

knead press or squeeze thoroughly

L

laborious requiring much physical effort

laconic using few words in writing or speech

lament express regret

languid lacking in liveliness or spirit; dreamy

laud praise, glorify, or honor

lavish giving or using a large amount of something

lethargic fatigue; feeling abnormal drowsiness or weariness

levity humor

levy impose or collect; seize

lexicon vocabulary

lithe moving or bending with ease

litigious eager or prone to engaging in lawsuits

loath unwilling; reluctant

loathe great dislike or disgust

lofty rising to a great height

loquacious talkative

lucrative profitable

luminary (1) prominent or brilliant person (2) body that gives light

luminous glowing brightly; radiant

M

magnanimous noble; generous in spirit

malicious having or showing a desire to do harm

malleable easily influenced; changeable

marred ruined the beauty or perfection of

materialism concerned with giving importance to possessions

methodical careful and organized

meticulous accurate; exact

mirthful merry

miserly (1) hesitating to spend money; (2) small amount

mitigate make less severe

morose unhappy

mundane dull and ordinary

N

nascent just begun; in early stages of development

nefarious extremely wicked

negate to cause to be ineffective

neophyte beginner

nocturnal belonging to or active during the night

nonchalance act of not caring; being indifferent

notoriety condition of being well-known for something bad

novelty quality or state of being new

nurture take care of; help grow, develop, or succeed

O

obliterate wipe out

oblivion state of being unconscious, unaware, or forgotten

obscure not well-known

obsolete no longer in use

obstinate stubborn

obtuse unintelligent or stupid

ocular of or related to the eye

odious hateful

official (1) v. relating to an office or position; (2) n. one who holds such a position

officious kind; dutiful

olfactory of or related to the sense of smell

ominous foreshadowing evil; foreboding

onus burden or responsibility

opaque (1) not letting light through; (2) difficult to understand or explain

opportunist someone who tries to gain advantage through a situation

optimistic looking for or expecting good things to happen

opulence being superior in quality; rich

orator someone who excels at making speeches

oscillate swing or move back and forth

osculate kiss

ossified become fixed or rigid

ostentatious showy; conspicuous

P

pacifist someone who opposes war

palpable easily perceived or felt

panacea remedy for all diseases and ills; a "cure-all"

parsimony stinginess

partisan enthusiastic proponent of a belief or idea; committed to a political party

perfidy treachery; betrayal

periphery outside edge of an area

permutation transformation

perpetuate cause to continue

perspicacious having keen insight; perceptive

pervasive existing in every part of something

pessimism someone who looks for or expects bad things to happen

phenomenon remarkable development or event

philanthropy good deeds; efforts to increase the good of mankind

pittance very small sum

placate cause to calm

ponderous boring or dull; slow or awkward because of weight or size

posterity future generations; descendents

potentate sovereign or monarch

pragmatic reasonable and logical

preclude prevent something from happening

precocious having or showing qualities of an adult at a young age

presumptuous assuming too much

pretentious wanting to appear more successful or important than one really is

prevalent accepted, done, or happening over a large area

primeval original; having existed in the beginning

prodigal carelessly or foolishly wasting money or time

profusion large amount

progenitor ancestor

prolific producing a large amount

prosperity good fortune; success

prototype original work or standard used as an example for others

provincial limited; unsophisticated

proximity closeness

prudent exercising discretion and sound judgment

purvey supply or sell

Q

qualified having necessary skills, experience, or knowledge

quandary confusing predicament; perplexity

queue line of people waiting in order of arrival

quintessence most essential part

quixotic foolishly and impractically romantic

R

rancor angry feeling of dislike or hatred

rapport harmony; mutual understanding

rapturous extremely happy; euphoric

ratify make official

recluse someone who lives alone and avoids others

reconcile come to terms; bring back together; make compatible

rectify fix or correct

redundant unnecessary

refute disprove

relegate make lower or less important

remedial intended to improve or correct

renounce formally give up or no longer accept something

repose peaceful and tranquil rest

reprehensible deserving of strong criticism

reprove correct, usually in a gentle way

repudiate refuse to accept

resigned feeling or showing acceptance of something unpleasant

resplendent glowing

reticence act of being reserved or restrained; reluctant to talk or draw attention

retract take or bring back

reverent showing much respect

rife abundant

rigor difficult or unpleasant circumstances; being careful, strict, or exact

robust strong and healthy

ruminate contemplate; reflect on or remember something

S

sagacious wise; shrewd

salient prominent; standing or projecting outward

sanction official permission or approval

sanguine cheery

sapient acutely wise and insightful

satirical using humor to show political or societal faults

saturate (1) make very wet; (2) fill completely

scanty very small in size or amount

schism division

scintilla faint trace or spark

scrupulous doing only what is right or proper; having moral integrity

scrutinize examine closely

seclusion placing or keeping away from people

servile very obedient; trying hard to please

sinuous winding or bending; curving in and out

skeptic someone who questions or doubts

solvent capable of meeting financial obligations

sparse thin, not thick

sporadic often but not readily or steadily

squander waste

stagnant inactive; not changing or progressing

static unchanging; stationary

stringent strict

submissive willing to obey someone else

subordinate in a position of less power or authority; less important

subside become less strong or intense

subsidiary something that is subordinate or supplemental

substantiate prove the truth of something

succinct using few words; brief

succumb to give in to or fall under the influence of something

supercilious arrogant or haughty

superfluous more than what is necessary or sufficient

supplant take the place of; serve as a substitute for

surpass be better or greater than something

surreptitious stealthy or secret

susceptible easily affected or influenced

sycophant someone who praises powerful people to get approval

synthesis combination into a complex whole

T

taciturn quiet; not inclined to speak

tantamount equivalent in value, effect, or significance

tedious dull; boring

tenacity strength; firmness

terrestrial of or relating to earth or land

terse brief or direct in a way that may seem rude

theoretical based on theory or hypothesis rather than practical knowledge

tirade long, angry speech

tome large, usually scholarly, book

tortuous twisting and turning; devious or indirect tactics

torturous unpleasant or painful

tractable easily controlled

tranquil peaceful or calm

transgress go over a limit; violate

transient briefly passing through

travesty parody or poor imitation

tremulous fearful

truculent harsh; aggressively ferocious

turmoil confusion or disorder

turpitude depravity

U

ubiquitous present everywhere

ultimate most remote; last; best or most extreme

uninterested indifferent; not interested

unrelenting never giving up

usurp seize by force

V

vacillate changing repeatedly

vacuous lacking serious thought or intelligence

vapid dull or boring; uninteresting

variegated multicolored

vehement showing strong, angry feelings

venal capable of being bought; corrupt through bribery

venerable respected and revered; august

venerate feel or show deep respect

venial minor; pardonable

veracity truth or accuracy

verbose wordy

vestige trace of something lost or gone

viable workable; able to grow

vigor strength or determination

vilify say or write harsh or critical things

vindicate (1) prove that someone is not guilty; (2) show that something is true

vitriolic characterized by harsh or angry words

vituperative scathing; venomous

vivacious lively; spirited

vociferous blatant; conspicuous and offensive outcry

volatile explosive

W

wane decrease in size; dwindle

wanton lewd or lustful

wary careful; watchful

wily sly or crafty

winsome charming

wizened dry; shrunken; wrinkled

wrath vengeful anger

Z

zealot fanatical person

zeitgeist cultural, intellectual or moral tendencies of an era

zenith culminating or highest point

zephyr soft, gentle wind